Tibetan Buddhism: A Very Short Introduction

VERY SHORT INTRODUCTIONS are for anyone wanting a stimulating and accessible way in to a new subject. They are written by experts and have been published in more than 25 languages worldwide.

The series began in 1995 and now represents a wide variety of topics in history, philosophy, religion, science, and the humanities. The VSI library now contains more than 300 volumes—a Very Short Introduction to everything from ancient Egypt and Indian philosophy to conceptual art and cosmology—and will continue to grow in a variety of disciplines.

Very Short Introductions available now:

Available soon:

For more information visit our web site

www.oup.co.uk/general/vsi/

Matthew T. Kapstein

TIBETAN BUDDHISM

A Very Short Introduction

OXFORD
UNIVERSITY PRESS

Oxford University Press is a department of the University of Oxford.
It furthers the University's objective of excellence in research,
scholarship, and education by publishing worldwide.

Oxford   New York
Auckland   Cape Town   Dar es Salaam   Hong Kong   Karachi
Kuala Lumpur   Madrid   Melbourne   Mexico City   Nairobi
New Delhi   Shanghai   Taipei   Toronto

With offices in
Argentina   Austria   Brazil   Chile   Czech Republic   France   Greece
Guatemala   Hungary   Italy   Japan   Poland   Portugal   Singapore
South Korea   Switzerland   Thailand   Turkey   Ukraine   Vietnam

Oxford is a registered trademark of Oxford University Press
in the UK and certain other countries.

Published in the United States of America by
Oxford University Press
198 Madison Avenue, New York, NY 10016

Library of Congress Cataloging-in-Publication Data
Kapstein, Matthew.
Tibetan Buddhism : a very short introduction / Matthew T. Kapstein.
pages   cm
Includes bibliographical references and index.
ISBN 978-0-19-973512-9 (pbk. : alk. paper)
1. Buddhism—Tibet Region. I. Title.
BQ7604.K37   2013
294.3'923—dc23   2013006676

Printed by Integrated Books International, United States of America
on acid-free paper

Contents

List of illustrations

All photographs © Matthew T. Kapstein

Acknowledgments

The need for a concise introduction to Tibetan Buddhism has been felt for some time. I am grateful to Cynthia Read, my editor at Oxford University Press, for encouraging me to write one. Thanks, too, to Professor Bryan Cuevas (Florida State University) and one anonymous reader for their thoughtful comments on an earlier draft of the book, which were most helpful to me in preparing this version. I am also indebted to Charlotte Steinhardt and Joellyn Ausanka at OUP for their editoral interventions, facilitating and smoothing the passage from manuscript to published work.

Languages and pronunciation

As is inevitable in writing about Tibetan Buddhism, the
present work introduces many names and terms in Sanskrit
and Tibetan, languages that are not familiar to many readers.
Sanskrit, the ancient Indian language of learning, is written
phonetically according to the International Alphabet of Sanskrit
Transliteration. For Tibetan, I use the simplified system of the
Tibetan and Himalayan Library, modified on some occasions
to better accord with Tibetan pronunciation. Space does not
permit the inclusion of exact transcriptions according to Tibetan
spelling conventions, but readers requiring these may consult the
Tibetan spelling list at the conclusion of my *The Tibetans* (Oxford:
Blackwell, 2006). Here are some basic points for those who are
new to these languages:

- In both Sanskrit and Tibetan, the vowels *a, i, u, e,* and *o* are
  pronounced roughly as in Italian. The use of the macron (*ā*
  etc.) indicates lengthening of the vowel, not a change of quality.
  Sanskrit includes two diphthongs—*ai* (like *ie* in *pie*) and *au* (like
  ow in *now*)—while Tibetan adds the two vowels *ö* and *ü*, both as
  in German. Sanskrit *ṃ* indicates nasalization of the preceding
  vowel, similar to the final *n* in French words such as *bon*.

- In both Sanskrit and Tibetan, *h* following a consonant is a
  sign of aspiration (breathiness): *ph* is a breathy *p*, not an *f*, and

similarly *th* is a breathy *t*, not the *th* of English *think* or *this*. Dots underneath consonants in Sanskrit words indicate that the tongue is pointed to the roof of the mouth when they are uttered. *S* with either an accent (*ś*) or a dot (*ṣ*) is pronounced roughly *sh*. In Tibetan, *z* and *zh* sound to us more like *s* and *sh*, but with an accompanying low tone. *Ng* resembles the final sound in *song*, though English speakers find it hard to pronounce at the beginning of a word, as it often is in Tibetan.

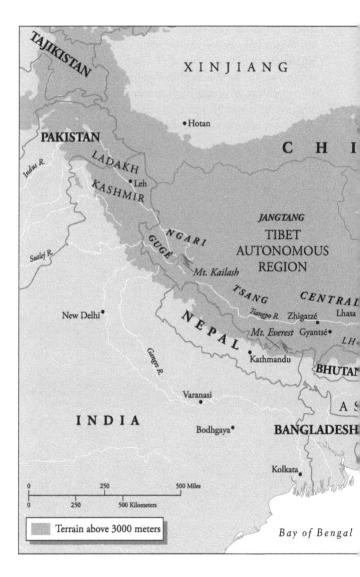

Chapter 1
The world of gods, demons, and men

One early spring day in the mid-1970s, at the residence of a Tibetan lama in the remote mountains of Nepal, I was invited to take tea and to converse with my learned host on the challenging topic of the nature of consciousness in Buddhist philosophy. As we pondered a difficult passage from an eighth-century Indian text, asserting that the mind cannot be an object to itself, we were abruptly interrupted by the lama's servant. He whispered to the teacher that a local couple had arrived with urgent business; could he please usher them in? Consent was granted and the couple, peasants who had some herds that they tended in the pastures above the monastery, entered, pallid and visibly quaking with fear. The night before a demon had entered their cattle shed, kicking up sparks and crackling, and almost provoked a stampede. What evil deed had they committed to become the objects of such demonic fury? And now that the bane was upon them, how was it to be appeased? Prostrating themselves before the lama, they begged for his protection and placed a small handful of cash on his table as an offering, together with a bowl brimming with fresh curds from their cows.

The lama immediately sought to put their minds at ease; seating them, he called for tea and biscuits to be served. After having them repeat in detail what had transpired—and by now I thought I recognized within the demonic attack an occurrence of the strange

meteorological phenomenon sometimes called "ball lightning"—
he took up his astrological almanac. Studying it for some minutes,
he rolled the divination dice he always kept close at hand and
counted off numerological combinations on his rosary. After
what must have seemed an eternity to the terrified couple, he
leaned forward and addressed them in the soothing tones of a
parent comforting a frightened child: There are no indications
that anything grave has occurred; your livestock will be fine,
he explained, neither you nor your children will be afflicted
with demon-borne sickness or similar ills. Only a passing
disturbance of the elements, due to minor faults of past karma,
is at stake. To purify your karma and to pacify these troubles, you
must undertake to practice each day the rite of *sang*—incense
fumigation dedicated to the spirits of the environment—and to
recite *Oṃ maṇipadme hūṃ*, the mantra of Avalokiteśvara, the
bodhisattva of compassion, one thousand times. Do this and
your problems will vanish. Above all, do not be afraid. Keep faith.
Adhere to compassion. You and those close to you will surely soon
be free from all that has caused this distress.

The lama then gave them knotted "protection cords," some
consecrated pills, a sip of perfumed water, and touching each on
the crown of the head, recited some prayers on their behalf. The
couple, still nervous but braving hopeful expressions, took their
leave. The lama looked up, smiled gently, and said, "Where were
we? 'Mind cannot see mind,' wasn't it?"

Religion's two ends

Tibetan Buddhism, as it is presented in the West, is often treated
as an erudite spiritual discipline, a world of subtle philosophy
and high-powered techniques of abstract meditation, dispensing
a bounty of insight and compassion to all. Although this
representation has its basis in the image that Tibetan Buddhism
has carefully crafted of itself through the centuries, for Tibetans
generally, including the social and religious elites, avoiding bad

karma and demonic disturbances, and undertaking meritorious rites and purifications were the fundamental objectives of religious life. Far from seeking to transcend the world in attainments of mystical contemplation, the day-to-day concerns that motivated the religious lives of most Tibetans—laymen and clergy alike—were the problems inherent in maintaining, not transcending, the order of the world by ensuring that harvests were plentiful, cattle productive, children sound, and enemies, whether demonic or human, impotent. Religious professionals, accordingly, were expected to minister to these and similar needs, whatever they might have to say about recondite topics like the nature of mind. Where the two ends of Tibetan religion—world-maintenance and world-transcendence—met was in the ideal of the *lama*, the spiritually accomplished teacher, often regarded as a bodhisattva who, in virtue of his superior compassion, learning, and ritual virtuosity, was both motivated and prepared to act in the service of the world at large. It goes without saying that not all who were titled *lama* in fact fulfilled this lofty ideal, though many surely strove to do so.

The bread-and-butter concerns of the Tibetan Buddhist clergy required that they devote considerable efforts to realizing the broad range of ritual demands for the protection, peace, and prosperity of their patrons, and to furnishing them with divinations and astrological consultations. In encountering Tibetan Buddhism as it is presented in many works on religious teaching, which tend to emphasize doctrines and contemplative practices, one rarely finds even oblique references to these ubiquitous aspects of Tibetan religion as it is lived. Not surprisingly, there has been a marked discrepancy between descriptions of Tibetan Buddhism based primarily on doctrinal texts and those derived from anthropological studies of life in traditional Tibetan and Himalayan communities. This introduction, though stressing the textual record of history, doctrine, and practice, nevertheless also attempts to recall pertinent "facts on the ground" as these are known from observing the actual religious life of Tibet.

Writings on Tibetan religion sometimes distinguish sharply
between Buddhism, originally an Indian religion that came to
dominate Tibetan culture from the late first millennium on, and
Bön, described as the ancient, indigenous religion of Tibet. This
characterization is not without its problems, however, and it will
be one of the tasks for the chapters that follow to provide greater
precision about this. For the moment, though, it should be noted
that the canonical scriptures of the Bön religion, in contrast to
those of mainstream Tibetan Buddhism, have much to say about
the world-maintaining facets of Tibetan religious life as these
have been in fact practiced. Accordingly, it is worthwhile to attend
in brief to what Bön sources have to say about this. It must be
constantly borne in mind that these matters are no less relevant to
Tibetan Buddhism, despite the latter's relative theological silence
about them. In practice, adherents of both Bön and Buddhism are
equally concerned with maintaining harmony with local spirits
and demons, with avoiding spiritual pollution and acquiring
tokens imbued with blessings of auspicious good fortune, and with
rites of passage that begin when a lama whispers a name into an
infant's ear and conclude with one's departure at death.

1. A senior monk explains the results of a divination (*mo*), calculated
on his rosary, to a young novice.

Between gods and demons

"In recognizing appearance to be a divinity (*lha*), and thus beneficent, or a demon (*dré*), and thus harmful, one comes to realize that all of birth and death are fashioned by divinities and demons (*lhadré*)." In these words, a twelfth-century Bön text summarizes the human predicament in its most essential features. We inhabit a world in which invisible powers, capable of helping or hurting us, are omnipresent. It is therefore imperative that we recognize these powers for what they are and learn how best to determine our own course in relation to them. The same work explains in brief how one deals with malefic spirits, which are regarded as perfectly analogous to the causes of disease.

Nor are the worldly divinities, in contrast to the implacable demons, considered as inherently well-disposed to human beings. They are characterized as often arrogant and vengeful but nevertheless "respectful of Bön and attached to the Shen [the Bön priesthood]." The relation the latter seek to form with these proud and powerful beings is therefore one of mastery and coercion, "for just as a master puts a slave to work, the practitioner, like the master, realizes [the deities] and their factotums to be like slaves and servants."

Despite the explicit mention of Bön and its priesthood here, these words may be applied in mainstream Buddhist contexts as well. Padmasambhava, the famed Indian master who visited Tibet during the eighth century and is believed to have played a cardinal role in the implantation there of Buddhism, legendarily converted many of the "arrogant" Tibetan divinities to Buddhism, coercing them to act as protectors of the foreign religion. Numbers of later Buddhist masters then followed his example. We read, for instance, of an eleventh-century adept, Zurchungpa, who vanquished the *lu* (nāgas, or serpent-demons) in the vicinity of his teacher Zurpoché's temple, forcing them to produce a tribute of *chang*, the rich barley ale that was a staple of the Tibetan diet:

On dealing with demons and disease

Living beings are subject to many sorts of affliction due to spirits and the like. One practices in order to remove these afflictions by means of divination and exorcism. Because beings are subject to many diseases of fever and chill, etc., one enters the way in order to alleviate those illnesses by medicine and treatment. When the effects of disease or afflicting spirits have appeared, one investigates what harm has occurred and what sort of disease or afflicting spirit is present. You diagnose a disease by examining pulse and urine, while afflicting spirits are investigated by means of divination and omens. Without halting the application of medicine and treatment to the effects of disease, you seek to bring about benefits; and without halting their application to the effects of afflicting spirits, you seek to bring about benefits through various divinations and exorcisms. This is the way of practical action. The view realized here resembles that of a scout on a mountain pass who spies out all enemies and dangers, and so brings about their avoidance or removal. Similarly, in this case you realize, with respect to disease, that it may be treated and cured, and with respect to afflicting spirits, that they may be impeded and deflected.

from *The Commentary of the Four Clever Men*

Zurchungpa intentionally summoned the sister of the nāga-demon who dwelt on the rock at Yazé Trakdzong. A thin snake appeared, which Zurchungpa turned into a fair lady by means of his gaze. At that Zurpoché said, "I want you to make the ale for the consecration of my temple."

The resulting ale was said to flow without limit.

Though few Tibetans presume to coerce the spirits in this way, to live, so far as is possible, in harmony with the "gods and demons" is nevertheless the concern of all. In one village I visited, I learned that several households had recently experienced a string of misfortunes, giving rise to collective worries in regard to the well-being of the village as a whole. When the leading lama in the region was consulted about it, he determined that the particular *lu* associated with the village spring was displeased, his shrine having been left to fall into disrepair and thus desecrated. The shrine of the *lu* was accordingly cleansed, refurbished, and consecrated anew, the rites being performed by Buddhist monks from the lama's monastery.

In short, without the cooperation of the local spirits, the community cannot hope to achieve prosperity; without the prosperity of the community, the material basis for religious achievement is lost; and without achievement in religious practice and learning, the cooperation of the local spirits cannot be won. This cycle of interdependence undergirds the religious life of Tibet in all its aspects, whether in settings denoted as Buddhist or Bön, whether on the level of the modest village or, in past times, of the Tibetan State under the leadership of the Dalai Lamas.

A rite of purification

The divine and demonic fauna of Tibet are remarkably diverse and prolific. One finds, accordingly, an abundant body of techniques— ritual and divinatory—deployed in the constant struggle required in order to sustain the balance of the spiritual ecology. Included here are practices as varied as pilgrimage, spirit-channeling, dramatic dances, and offerings of numerous kinds, and an elaborate material culture requiring the production of a great panoply of ritual objects including masks, prayer-flags, votive cakes, colorful thread-crosses, and much more. As an example of Tibet's "this worldly" religion, one specific, very common type of ritual may be considered: *sang*, or incense fumigation, the regular practice of which was urged upon the couple whose cattle fell victim to demonic attack.

2. A monk (*right*) and a layman perform *sang* on the Lamjura Pass in eastern Nepal.

Sang, literally "purification," is a ubiquitous Tibetan custom in which the fragrant smoke of juniper and other substances is offered to the gods and spirits pervading the land. The term *sang* may be etymologically related to another word, also pronounced *sang*, which forms part of the Tibetan term for the Enlightened One, the Buddha: *sang-gyé*. Here it refers to the Buddha's awakening as a sloughing off of the sleep of ignorance that characterizes the mundane world. *Sang* as fumigation, analogously, offers a cleansing fragrance to the spirits, purifying the taints of the environment that they find distasteful. The custom is almost certainly of indigenous origin in Tibet and adjacent regions, and is practiced in one form or another by virtually all Tibetans, monks and laypersons, men and women, rich and poor. One of the great annual festivals, *Dzamling chisang*, performed in the early summer on the full-moon day of the fifth lunar month, is its greatest elaboration, offering, literally, a "general fumigation (on behalf of all the spirits) of the world." In settled villages, many houses will have a special furnace, a *sangtab*, placed on the roof or in the courtyard for the regular performance of *sang*, while at long-term

8

nomadic encampments such a furnace may be constructed outside the tents. It is an offering that in its most basic form is barely a ritual at all: one burns a bit of juniper while reciting a formula such as *lha gyel lo*, "the gods are victorious!" and perhaps a few mantras, like the ubiquitous *Oṃ maṇipadme hūṃ*.

Tibetan understandings of *sang* cohere closely with beliefs regarding the character of the local divinities, particularly the mountain gods. These are beings of great power but also olfactory sensitivity; it is for this reason, for instance, that there is a widespread cultural ban on grilling or roasting meat, which may bring about spiritual pollution, or *drip*. Although the already limited Tibetan culinary arts thereby suffer for this reason, raw, dried, or boiled meat (as in a stew or soup) are de rigueur, for the gods frown upon those who offend them with the stench of burning flesh. Sweet juniper smoke, however, they find suitable. Moreover, one must offer a particular type of juniper that does not spark or pop when it burns. Explosions, bright flashes, and sharp sounds disrupt the dignified tranquility of the divinities no less, as we have seen, than they do the peace of cattle and men. When they are well pleased, the gods become propitious, and the human community thrives under the resulting favorable auspices (*trashi*). The gods, irascible though they may be, are drawn to virtue (*gewa*) and to the merit (*sonam*) thereby accumulated. They shun evil and pollution (*dik-drip*).

The practice of *sang*, like virtually all that touches upon the cults of the Tibetan indigenous deities, came within the orbit of tantric Buddhism no later than the twelfth century and perhaps much earlier. The esoteric ritual scriptures, or tantras, of Indian Buddhism provided the ritual technology for sublimating and organizing autochthonous beliefs and practices in regard to all manner of spirits, divine or demonic, and so quickly pervaded both Buddhist and Bön milieux. Formalized liturgies for the performance of popular rites such as *sang* appeared, in which they were elaborated beyond the simple customs described earlier. Part of one such liturgy for the performance of *sang*, composed during the sixteenth century, reads as follows:

In a great vessel of diverse precious gems,
Are sacramental substances, worldly enjoyments,
Consecrated as gnostic ambrosia by three mantra-syllables.
This lively mix, an appealing offering, I dedicate
To the gurus, divinities, goddesses, and protectors . . .,
To the lords of our earth and the "guests" among the six classes to
      whom I'm indebted;
In particular, to those who steal life and longevity,
Elemental spirits bringing disease, demons, and obstacles,
And all types of bad dreams, evil signs and omens,
Irrascible spirits and lords of miraculous powers,
Creditors seeking food, abode and wealth,
Lords of pollution and madness, demons of death and their
      consorts,
Vampires and spirits of plague, demonesses of town and country,
As many as there are throughout the expanses of space.
May my sins and obscurations, accumulated throughout the three
      times,
My [illicit] enjoyment of the wealth of the saṅgha and of the
      deceased,
Be purified by this fire-offering.
May each particle of each flame, filling space,
Become an inexhaustible mass of good offerings
Pervading all the fields of the Buddhas.
May the gift of this offering in the flames, gnostic light,
Pervade the abodes of the six classes down to the lowest hell. . . .
And may all beings awaken as Buddhas in the heart of
      enlightenment!

This text addresses Tibetan religious experience on several levels. It seeks to appease and restore order to the "elemental spirits bringing disease, demons, and obstacles," while at the same time conferring gnosis—the realization of the Buddha's enlightenment—on all "abodes of the six classes"—gods, anti-gods, humans, animals, ghosts, and denizens of hell—inhabiting the round of rebirth, or *saṃsāra*. In its aspiration for the salvation of all beings, it adheres to the cardinal values of Mahāyāna Buddhism, while in its use of spell-like mantras to consecrate the juniper and other substances offered into the flames "as gnostic ambrosia" for the practice of *sang*, it adopts the ritual usages of Buddhist Tantra. It forms a tapestry of sorts, in which the Tibetan world of gods, demons, and men, the Mahāyāna Buddhist orientation to universal enlightenment, and the ritual technologies of Tantric esotericism are tightly interwoven. In actual practice, the varied themes that may be identified here are most often inseparable, forming for Tibetans a balanced whole, whose several parts, in both their historical and doctrinal aspects, are indissociable.

Chapter 2
Sources of Tibetan religious traditions

The introduction of Buddhism to Tibet

It is not clear when Tibetans first encountered the Buddhist religion. Tradition holds that it was in the time of Lha Totori (ca. fourth century CE), a ruler of Yarlung in southeastern Tibet: Buddhist scriptures and images are related to have miraculously fallen upon his palace, though others say they were offered by a wandering Central Asian Buddhist monk. Although these are legends, it is not implausible that elements of Buddhism arrived during this period of Tibetan prehistory; Tibet was then surrounded by lands in which Buddhism was a long-established religious and cultural system: Nepal and India to the south, China to the east, the Silk Road states to the north, and the pre-Islamic Iranian world to the west.

Tibetan history begins with the Tsenpo, or emperor, Songtsen Gampo (ca. 617–49), who militarily and politically unified the Tibetan plateau and began the conquest of surrounding lands. The Tibetan system of writing, based on Indian models, was developed at this time. The emperor's marriage to the Chinese princess Wencheng (d. 680) is believed to have been accompanied by the installation in his capital city, Lhasa, of a precious image of Śākyamuni Buddha brought from China as part of her dowry and said to have been manufactured in

India as a portrait of the Buddha himself. The statue, known as the Jowo ("Lord") remains Tibet's holiest object of pilgrimage. Later accounts relate that the monarch also married a Nepalese Buddhist princess, Bhṛkuṭī, and that inspired by his two foreign queens, he and his court embraced the Indian religion. Indeed, Songtsen Gampo would be eventually regarded as a Tibetan emanation of the regal bodhisattva of universal compassion, Avalokiteśvara, or Chenrezi in Tibetan, who was believed to have been entrusted by the Buddha Śākyamuni with the task of converting Tibet.

Although Songtsen Gampo extended some degree of tolerance to Buddhism, at least in order to accommodate his foreign brides, it is unlikely that the alien faith made much progress in Tibet before another half century or more had passed. Under the king Tri Düsong (d. 704) a temple was founded in the region of Ling, in far eastern Tibet, perhaps in connection with military campaigns in the southeastern part of the Tibetan empire against the Buddhist kingdom of Nanzhao (modern Yunnan). During the reign of Tri Düsong's successor Tri Detsuktsen (704–55), there is clear evidence for renewed Buddhist advances in Central Tibet. Once again, it was a Chinese princess who played an instrumental role in supporting the faith.

Princess Jincheng arrived in Tibet in 710, two years before her then six-year-old husband-to-be was granted the title of Tsenpo. She is said to have been much saddened by the absence of Buddhist funerary rites for deceased nobility and so introduced the Chinese Buddhist custom of memorializing the dead during seven weeks of mourning. This practice promoted the belief, later famed in such works as the so-called *Tibetan Book of the Dead*, that forty-nine days typically intervene between death and rebirth. The princess also invited Khotanese monks to Central Tibet, who formed the first community of the saṅgha in that land. However, following Jincheng's death in 739, probably due to the plague, there was a sharp anti-Buddhist reaction and the foreign monks were expelled.

The last years of Tri Detsuktsen's rule were marked by grave factional conflict among the nobility, culminating in the monarch's assassination. When his thirteen-year-old son was placed on the throne in 755, factions hostile to Buddhism dominated the court. The young Tsenpo, Tri Songdetsen (742–ca. 802), nevertheless became imperial Tibet's greatest ruler and an unparallelled Buddhist benefactor. In his surviving edicts, we are told that early in his reign Tibet faced severe epidemics afflicting both humans and livestock. When no viable solution appeared, he rescinded the ban on the practice of Buddhist rites that had been in force since his father's dethronement, and matters rapidly improved. As a result, he adopted Buddhism and undertook to study its teachings in depth. His conversion took place in 762, when he was twenty.

An emperor's conversion

The testimony offered by the edicts and other writings attributed to Tri Songdetsen suggest that he acquired a keen interest in Buddhist doctrine, key elements of which he summarizes in these words: "Those who are born and revolve among the four sorts of birth, from beginningless origins to the infinite end, become as they are owing to their deeds [lé, Sanskrit karman]. . . . The results of one's deeds ripen upon oneself. One may be born as a god among the heavenly stages, or as a human on earth, or as an anti-god, a hungry ghost, an animal, or a subterranean creature of the hells—all born in these six [realms] have done so owing to their own deeds.

"Transcending the world are those who become Buddhas, and those who make progress as bodhisattvas, self-awakened ones [Skt. pratyekabuddha], or pious disciples [Skt. śrāvaka]—all of them have done so owing to the provisions of merit and gnosis that they themselves have amassed."

Besides his affirmation of Buddhist teachings of the painful cycle of rebirth—saṃsāra (khorwa in Tibetan)—and its termination in the realization of a Buddha's enlightenment, or *nirvāṇa* (*nyangdé*), it is striking that Tri Songdetsen was also particularly interested in how we may *know* the truth of religious claims. For he adds: "If one investigates what is found in the Dharma [the Buddha's teaching], some points are immediately evident in their good or evil consequences, while others that are not immediately evident may nevertheless be inferred on the basis of those which are, and so are also fit to be held with certainty."

Thus, he became familiar with, and sought to introduce his subjects to, the basics of Indian Buddhist philosophy, which holds that knowledge may have two valid sources (Skt. *pramāṇa*): direct perception (Skt. *pratyakṣa*) of what is evident to the senses and intellectual intuition, and inference (Skt. *anumāna*) of what is "hidden," that is, not directly evident. In later times, the investigation of these sources of knowledge would be a focal point of monastic education.

Tri Songdetsen founded Tibet's first Buddhist monastery, Samyé (ca. 779) and invited the Indian teacher Śāntarakṣita to ordain the first officially sanctioned Tibetan Buddhist monks. Henceforth, the Tibetan Buddhist monastic community would follow the Vinaya, or monastic code, of the Indian Mūlasarvāstivāda order to which Śāntarakṣita adhered. The translation of Buddhist canonical scriptures was also sponsored by the court on a massive scale. The accomplishments of the Tibetan imperial translation committees, in terms of both quantity and precision, may be counted among the summits of the art of translation at any place or time. Tibetan translators, in collaboration with Indian and Central Asian Buddhist scholars, created a rigorous Sanskrit-Tibetan lexicon to guide their work, one result being a standardized doctrinal and philosophical vocabulary in Tibetan. The translators also composed manuals introducing the newly coined vocabulary together with elements of Buddhist thought. The creation of a Tibetan canonical literature was continued under Tri Songdetsen's successors until the collapse of the dynasty during the mid-ninth century. By that time, many hundreds of Indian religious and philosophical writings had been translated. The Tibetan Buddhist canon, organized during the fourteenth century into the complementary collections of the *Kanjur* ("translated scriptures") and *Tanjur* ("translated commentaries"), and occupying more than three hundred large volumes, preserves numerous Indian as well as some Chinese texts now unavailable elsewhere.

The foundation of Samyé monastery is also said to have involved the intercession of Padmasambhava, a renowned tantric adept from Oḍḍiyāna in northwestern India, who was required to quell the hostile spirits and divinities of Tibet in order to win their allegiance to Buddhism. Whatever his actual role may have been at the time, Padmasambhava would become the object of considerable devotion and was eventually deified as the "Precious Guru" (Guru Rinpoché) of the Tibetan people as a whole. Together, the king Tri Songdetsen, the monk Śāntarakṣita, and the adept Padmasambhava are revered as the trinity of the Tibetan conversion. They represent three of the major constituents of the Tibetan Buddhist world: royal lay patron, ordained monk, and tantric adept.

It is sometimes thought that the adoption of Buddhism by the Tibetan court pacified the warlike Tibetan people and thus, having emasculated the nation, brought about the decline and fall of its empire. It is clear, however, that Tibet continued aggressive policies long after adopting Buddhism as an aspect of Tibetan imperial ideology. Buddhism provided the empire with the symbolic means to represent itself as the worldly embodiment of a universal spiritual and political order, a "cosmocracy" so to speak, in which the Tsenpo was the Buddha's earthly representative. This was made tangible through the Tsenpo's identification with the cosmic Buddha of Radiant Light, Vairocana, whose icon was widely reproduced in imperial domains.

Tibetan Buddhism

16

3. Padmasambhava, with his Indian and Tibetan consorts Mandaravā and Yeshé Tsogyel, in the "speaking image" revealed as spiritual treasure (*terma*) at Yarlung Sheldrak.

Two views of enlightenment

The Buddhist teachings favored by the Tibetan monarchy represented the traditions of the great northern Indian monastic universities, above all Nālandā, with which Śāntarakṣita was affiliated. At these establishments, the monastic code of the Vinaya formed the basis for monastic life among the inmates, both novices (Skt. *śramaṇera*, Tib. *getsül*) and fully ordained monks (Skt. *bhikṣu*, Tib. *gelong*). Laymen and -women were connected with the monastery as devotees and patrons, and ordained laymen (Skt. *upāsaka*, Tib. *genyen*) might also take up monastic residence in order to further religious pursuits. The vows of these grades— laymen and -women, novice men and women, monks and nuns— were known as *prātimokṣa*, an expression sometimes understood to mean "individual liberation." The *prātimokṣa* vows required

17

abstinence from intentional killing, theft, falsehood, intoxication, and sexual misconduct, understood in the case of novices, monks, and nuns to prohibit all sexual activity. The monastic life of novices was regulated by a small number of additional vows, while those who were fully ordained had more than two hundred rules by which they were bound. Though this pattern was maintained in Tibet, many of the detailed rules of the Vinaya—for instance, the prohibition of an evening meal following the major meal at midday—came to be quietly neglected.

A well-motivated aspirant adhering to the *prātimokṣa* could strive to achieve learning and insight through study and meditation. Here, the Indian tradition as it became known in Tibet favored a gradual training, sometimes considered as comprising "three vehicles." These were already referred to in the edicts of Tri Songdetsen and became fundamental for all later formulations of Tibetan Buddhist doctrine.

A ninth-century translator on Buddhism's "three vehicles"

The "three vehicles" were carefully summarized in the treatise *Distinctions of Views* (*Tawé Khyepar*) by Yeshé-dé, a leading translator at Samyé monastery. He begins with the concept of a "vehicle":

"'Vehicle' is similar to 'conveyance.' It is a vehicle because, conveyed by it, you reach your proper abode, and because, like a bridge, a boat, or a ship, when you are conveyed by and rely upon it, you traverse the torrent of saṃsāra.

"You enter the vehicle of the pious disciples [Skt. *śrāvaka*] through the four truths: (1) The five bundles [Skt. *skandha*, i.e., form, sensation, perception, volitions, and consciousness] . . . are the ground of various sufferings; so at first there is the realization of the truth of suffering; (2) Then, when the cause of suffering is

realized to arise from deeds [Skt. *karman*] and afflictions
[Skt. *kleśa*], you realize the truth of the origination [of suffering];
(3) Next, abandoning deeds and afflictions, you leave off the five
bundles and understand [the resulting peace] to be true, thus
realizing the truth of cessation (= nirvāṇa); (4) Then, concerning
the means to attain cessation, you understand this to be the
sublime path that includes right views, etc., and so realize the
truth of the path. When corrupted and uncorrupted [phenomena]
are reduced to cause and result, you see that there is no self that
is agent or enjoyer, and so realize the selflessness [Skt. *anātman*]
of the individual. Saṃsāra is inexhausible trouble, while nirvāṇa is
understood to be peace and happiness.

"Concerning the vehicle of the self-awakened ones
[Skt. *pratyekabuddha*], you enter it through the twelve limbs of
dependent origination [Skt. *pratītyasamutpāda*]. Having seen the
evil consequence of saṃsāra to be old age and death, you examine
whence these arise and discover their basis to be birth. Pursuing
the inquiry, you proceed until reaching ignorance, realizing [each
step] as cause and result. When [all experience] is reduced to
dependent origination, you see that there is neither 'I' nor 'mine,'
hence no individual self. Ignorance may therefore be terminated,
and, when it is, you see [the successive limbs of dependent
origination] terminated through to old age and death. . . . Turning
to purification, you practice such virtues as the perfections in
order to find enlightenment and nirvāṇa for yourself alone, but
without much compassion; because you do not act on behalf of
many sentient beings, this is called the vehicle of the
self-awakened ones.

"In the greater vehicle (Mahāyāna), you know that ultimately all
entities are insubstantial and realize that saṃsāra and nirvāṇa are
not two, while, relatively, entities are objectified as apparitional.
Thus you are endowed with discernment as well as great
compassion. Neither abandoning saṃsāra nor appropriating

19

nirvāṇa, you act for the sake of all sentient beings according to
the ten transcendent perfections and so accomplish perfectly
the purposes of self and other. Attaining the ten levels of the
bodhisattva, together with the level of the Buddha, which is the
result, this is called the 'greater vehicle.'"

The teaching of the "three vehicles," accentuating the supreme
status of the Mahāyāna, provided a framework for subsequent
Tibetan elaborations of Buddhist doctrine. It emphasizes the
foundations of classical Indian Buddhism: (1) the Four Truths of
suffering, its cause, its cessation in nirvāṇa, and the path whereby
this is achieved; (2) the selflessness of the person; dependent
origination; and (3) the ultimate identity of saṃsāra and nirvāṇa in
the compassionate vision of the bodhisattva. In Tibet, as in India,
the conception of the Mahāyāna corresponded to a stage of spiritual
practice and not, as is sometimes mistakenly assumed, to a separate
order or sect of Buddhism. According to the Mahāyāna, the
bodhisattva was one who strived over countless lifetimes to achieve
the moral perfection and insight that is buddhahood. At the same
time, he or she was an ordained layperson, novice, monk, or nun,
and as such was also grounded in the spiritual training of the "pious
disciple," or *śrāvaka*. Only the category of the *pratyekabuddha* was
without a corresponding practical correlate and remained, to all
intents and purposes, merely a theoretical placeholder.

During the 780s Tri Songdetsen's armies conquered Dunhuang,
a major center of Chinese Buddhism, where teachers of Chan
(from Skt. *dhyāna*, "meditation"; Zen in Japanese) introduced
Tibetans to the idea that spiritual awakening was immediately,
intuitively present, without striving for innumerable lifetimes as
Indian Buddhism affirmed. One such teacher, the Chinese master
Moheyan, was invited to Central Tibet, where he gained a large
following, including members of the royal family. The popularity
of his teaching led to a protracted dispute between partisans of
"sudden" versus "gradual" enlightenment, the former sometimes

The confrontation of "sudden" and "gradual" at Samyé

When master Kamalaśīla asked for his opponent's position, saying, "What is the Chinese religious tradition like?" the Chinese responded, "Your religious tradition, beginning with going for refuge and the cultivation of an enlightened attitude, is an ascent from below, like a monkey climbing a tree. Because one will not be awakened as a Buddha by such contrived doctrines, it is in this tradition of ours, in which one contemplates the nonconceptual, that one becomes awakened by realizing the nature of mind. So this is like the eagle's alighting from the sky upon the top of a tree; it is a 'pure panacea' because it is a doctrine that thus descends from on high."

To this the master said, "Your example and its significance are both invalid. For the eagle alights upon the tree, either spontaneously generated in the sky with its wings fully grown, or born in its eyrie, where its wings have gradually matured. Only then does it alight. The first is an impossibility and the second should be a gradualist example, but is inappropriate as an example of sudden enlightenment."

from *The Testament of Ba*

associated with a doctrine of a radical breakthrough via mystical intuition, and the latter with the methodical application of reasoned analysis. The controversy resurfaced repeatedly in later times owing to its implications concerning spiritual progress and, indeed, our very nature: Are we essentially flawed creatures, for whom self-perfection is a distant goal, or are we already awakened Buddhas? Does the latter position entail a kind of gnosticism, according to which ignorance and knowledge are all that really matter, and moral effort merely an illusion?

Traditional sources recount that the first debate over these issues took place at Samyé during the late-eighth century, and that the disputants were master Moheyan and Śāntarakṣita's disciple, the Indian philosopher Kamalaśīla. The accounts that survive are late and tend to caricature the Chan perspective. The Samyé debate may have been a draw, but later tradition reviles Moheyan as representing an irrational doctrine of instant enlightenment and regards Kamalaśīla's emphasis upon the gradual cultivation of the moral and intellectual virtues of a bodhisattva as the enduring paradigm to be emulated by Tibetan Buddhists. Nevertheless, elements of the Chan teaching remained current in Tibet, and a Tibetan Chan lineage persisted in far eastern Tibet until at least the eleventh century.

The fall of the Tibetan empire

Under Tri Songdetsen's successors, Tri Desongtsen (r. 804–15) and Tri Relpachen (r. 815–38), Buddhist monasteries and schools flourished with royal support. In the reign of Üdumtsen (r. 838–42), better known as Lang Darma ("ox-youth," or "ox-dharma"), royal sponsorship of the monasteries was reduced or withdrawn, most likely owing to declining state revenues. Later histories, however, recount that this monarch was a devotee of the Bön religion who ruthlessly persecuted Buddhism until his assassination in 842 by the Buddhist monk Lhalung Pelgyi Dorjé. Although Pelgyi Dorjé was certainly a historical figure, he became the hero of a colorful legend celebrating the act of regicide he is supposed to have carried out. Disguised as a black-cloaked Bönpo sorcerer seeking to bless the ruler, he is said to have approached the king, only to shoot him with his ceremonial bow and arrow before escaping on a black stallion. His pursuers, wherever they searched, could not find a Bönpo rider on a black mount, but saw a Buddhist monk on a white horse. Lhalung Pelgi Dorjé had tinted its coat with charcoal and was wearing reversible robes. A quick plunge into a nearby river had been sufficient to return the horse's color to white while changing his own garb.

Whatever the truth may have been, the collapse of the Tibetan empire followed soon after Üdumtsen's death and the domains of his successors were gradually reduced to a collection of petty kingdoms. Tibet remained without central authority for the next four hundred years. Though much of Buddhist institutional activity was curtailed by the termination of imperial patronage, some traditions of study and practice survived, and the esoteric traditions of the Tantras appear to have flourished following the empire's fall, particularly around tenth-century Dunhuang. Monastic Buddhism, however, virtually disappeared in Central Tibet and was preserved among Tibetans primarily in the far east, in the modern Chinese provinces of Qinghai and Gansu. It was here, during the mid-tenth century, that a young Bönpo converted and received Buddhist ordination. Known to posterity as Lachen Gongpa Rapsel, the "great lama whose spirit was clear," he (or his disciples) later ordained a number of seekers from Central and Western Tibet, sparking a monastic revival movement that came to be called the "later promulgation of the teaching" (*tenpa chidar*). The consequences of this will be seen in the following chapter, but first we survey two developments contemporaneous with the decline of Buddhist monasticism: the emergence of the Bön religion and, simultaneously, that of a distinctive form of esoteric Buddhism, later to be known as Nyingmapa, the "ancient tradition."

The emergence of the Bön religion

Although "Bön" is often used as a designation for the pre-Buddhist Tibetan religion, the religious life of Tibet prior to the introduction of Buddhism remains poorly understood. Because the Tibetan system of writing was adopted just as Buddhism was becoming known, there are few records of early Tibetan religion in which Buddhist influences are altogether absent. From the existing texts, it is not even clear that there was a particular term regularly used to designate the pre-Buddhist Tibetan religion. In the first works in which the word *bön* is found, it refers not to a religion but to specific types of priests: the expression *durbön*, for instance, names those who were specialists in mortuary rituals (*dur*).

One early text in which "Bön" unambiguously denotes the pre-Buddhist religion is, significantly, a description of a debate following Tri Songdetsen's death. In this narrative, rival factions of priests dispute whether the late Tsenpo should be given a Buddhist or a Bön funeral, that is, a funeral according to ancestral traditions. As we know from Tibetan royal records, the last rites and interment of the Tsenpo and his kin were important affairs of state requiring long, complex preparations, including the mummification of the deceased and the construction of an elaborate mausoleum. The *durbön* just mentioned were among the principle officiants of these rites. The attempt by Buddhist monks to assume authority in this context therefore provoked the ire of hereditary priests who risked losing ancient prerogatives. The confrontation between Buddhism and Bön would be one of the enduring themes in later accounts of the reign of Tri Songdetsen, both Buddhist and Bönpo sources maintaining that the ruler expelled the Bön priesthood from Central Tibet.

The Bön religion that arose after the Tibetan empire fell, however, was not just the continuation of archaic beliefs and practices. It preserved much ancient lore, notably in its mortuary traditions, but was nevertheless a new religion in many respects, emerging from the confrontation between the older traditions and Buddhism. Evidence of this may be found in Bön doctrines, institutional forms, and spiritual disciplines.

Bön, like Buddhism, came to consider itself to be a foreign religion that had been introduced into Tibet from abroad; again like Buddhism, it held that it was founded by a Buddha, and that its highest goal was the Buddha's enlightened state. In short, the organized Bön religion appeared in many important respects to be a local form of Buddhism. This was underscored by the nomenclature adopted by the Bönpo, who spoke not of a contrast between Bön and Buddhism but between Bön and Chö, the latter term being Tibetan for Sanskrit "Dharma," understood as the doctrine, or teaching. Bön was thus a mirror of Buddhism: it originated not with the Indian Buddha Śākyamuni but with the Buddha Shenrab Miwo in Inner Asia ages ago. It was introduced to Tibet not from Nepal, China, and India during the late first millennium but via the western Tibetan kingdom of Zhangzhung long before. Like its rival, Chö, it created a canon of teachings embodied in voluminous scriptures, said to have been translated into Tibetan from the languages of Zhangzhung and elsewhere, and its adherents counted monastic clergy, tantric adepts, and laypersons.

The creation of the Bönpo scriptural canon encouraged the written redaction of autochthonous techniques and beliefs. Although Bönpo authors often employed Buddhist terminology, they also documented many practices traditionally governing Tibetan interactions with the spirit world in its benign and malignant aspects. In time, these ancient traditions, which sought not transcendence but mastery of the divine and demonic forces of the phenomenal world, would become part and parcel of Tibetan Buddhist thought and practice as well. The inclination toward holism and a view of the world as the play of divine and quasi-divine energies that we find within it would be regularly reasserted throughout the history of Tibetan religious thought. This was especially true of esoteric (or "tantric") Buddhism, which emphasized ritual agency and found its philosophical basis in the Mahāyāna conception of the ultimate identity of worldly existence (*saṃsāra*) and transcendent peace (*nirvāṇa*), eventually embracing, besides the Indian pantheon, the native gods and demons of Tibet.

Nyingmapa beginnings

Although we have mentioned tantric, or esoteric, Buddhism, we have so far left this undefined. In its essence, Buddhist tantra is an approach to Mahāyāna practice and not a separate "school." The tantras, esoteric scriptures, maintain that the progress of the bodhisattva, who strives for buddhahood throughout countless lifetimes, may be hastened through techniques of ritual and yoga revealed only to specially qualified disciples. These techniques begin with the initiation of the disciple into a divine realm schematically depicted as a maṇḍala, in which one is ritually purified, consecrated with divine attributes, and instructed in visualizing a divinity and reciting its mantra. Though thought to facilitate rapid progress, the ritual techniques of the tantras were considered to be possibly dangerous and disruptive. They were Mahāyāna teachings, to be sure, but in the wrong hands could undermine the Mahāyāna's insistence on the step-by-step achievement of moral perfection. Hence, though the Tsenpo Tri Songdetsen and his successors permitted some tantric practice in Tibet, they carefully restricted it, lest unqualified persons be misled. This was explicated in the ninth century by the Tsenpo Tri Desongtsen:

Tibetan Buddhism

> The tantras . . . are to be kept secret. It is not appropriate to explain and to teach them to the unqualified. Though it has been permitted to translate and to practice them, there have been those who have not deciphered what is expounded in them allusively, and seizing upon literal understanding have practiced perversely. . . . This being so, hereafter, it is not permitted to translate haphazardly the tantras of mantra and the mantra-terms except for those . . . that have been caused to be translated on order from above.

With the fall of the empire the imperial effort to control the dissemination of tantric Buddhism was undone, and free agency became the rule. Beyond the small number of tantras translated under royal authority, many additional tantras were circulated during the ninth and tenth centuries. Those adhering to these "former translations"—tantras introduced before the eleventh century—came to be known as Nyingmapa, the "ancients." Historically, the Nyingmapa asserted the preeminence of the Indian tantric master Padmasambhava, who was effectively deified. Other teachers of the eighth and ninth centuries, notably the Indian sage Vimalamitra and the Tibetan translator Vairocana, were also claimed as forebears. The teaching of these figures was considered to present the whole gamut of Buddhist doctrine and practice in nine sequential vehicles (*tekpa rimpa gu*), of which the last three, comprising the esoteric instructions of the highest tantras, represented the distinctive heritage of the Nyingmapa. The pinnacle of the system was the abstract and visionary approach to contemplation known as the Supreme Yoga (*atiyoga*), or Great Perfection (*dzokchen*), whose authenticity was often challenged in later times by adherents of the "new translations," the post-tenth century translations of tantric texts. From the twelfth century on, the Nyingmapa came to rely increasingly on new revelations, mostly of texts and teachings attributed to Padmasambhava, and referred to as "treasures" (*terma*). This permitted Nyangrel Nyima Özer (1124–96) and later "treasure-revealers" (*tertön*) to elaborate an abundant and influential body of ritual, historical, and legendary literature. Though widely contested, these contributed greatly to the formation of Tibetan religious culture.

The nine vehicles of the Nyingmapa and of Bön

The classical Buddhist idea of "three vehicles," combined with Tibetan numerology emphasizing the number nine, yielded nine vehicles as known in varied Nyingmapa and Bönpo traditions. Two prominent versions are those of Padmasambhava and of the "Southern Treasure" of the Bönpo.

Padmasambhava's *Garland of Views* teaches three "dialectical vehicles" and six "adamantine vehicles" (Skt. *vajrayāna*). The first are the classical vehicles of pious disciples, self-awakened ones, and bodhisattvas. The "adamantine vehicles" are tantric teachings, symbolized by the adamantine scepter, or *vajra* (Tib. *dorjé*), representing perfect clarity and indestructibility. These form two triads. First are the "exoteric" tantras: Kriyātantra (tantras of ritual action), Ubhayatantra (tantras partaking of both [rituals and austerities]), and Yogatantra (tantras stressing the austerities of yoga). Second are the "esoteric" Yogatantras: Great Yoga (*mahāyoga*), emphasizing creative visualization; Subsequent Yoga (*anuyoga*), focusing on the mastery of internal energies; and Supreme Yoga (*atiyoga*), the Great Perfection (*dzokchen*), disclosing the mind's ultimate nature.

A Bönpo system of nine vehicles was taught in the "Southern Treasure" revelations beginning in the eleventh century. There are four "causal vehicles," four "resultant vehicles," and one "Great Vehicle." The first four are all called *Shen*, meaning a "priestly way" and emphasizing mundane rituals: the Shen of Augury, stressing divination and exorcism of troubles caused by harmful spirits; the Shen of Appearance, elaborating rituals for negotiating human relations with demons and divinities; the Shen of Marvels, to coerce particularly savage spirits; and the Shen of Existence, codifying ancient mortuary rites.

The four "resultant vehicles" correspond to aspects of Buddhist teaching: the vehicle of laymen teaches moral precepts governing body, speech, and mind; the vehicle of ascetics, the Bönpo monastic tradition, stresses the cultivation of compassion; the vehicle of the Alpha Pure resembles the "exoteric" tantras of Buddhism; and the Primordial Shen is similar to the Buddhist Mahāyoga and Anuyoga.

Finally, the Great Vehicle is the Great Perfection, teaching the four qualities of oneness, plainness, openness, and spontaneity.

Although the Nyingmapa system of Padmasambhava and the Bön Southern Treasure are distinct in their treatment of the lower vehicles, they converge in their higher ranks, uniting at the apex.

Chapter 3

The growth of the orders and schools

Renewal in West Tibet

In the late tenth century, Tibet entered a new age of economic and political development. Local lords struggled for supremacy and religious authority was no less contested than temporal power. Seekers and adventurers looked for authoritative sources of Buddhist teaching in India and Nepal, traveling in search of gurus, scriptures, and esoteric lore. These trends were particularly prominent in western Tibet, where the translator Rinchen Zangpo (958–1055) was patronized by the devout monarch of the Gugé kingdom, Yeshé-ö (ca. 959–1036). This figure, who, in an exception to monastic tradition requiring ordination within an established lineage, ordained himself as a monk, wished to purify Tibetan Buddhism from what he regarded as corrupt forms of tantrism that had emerged during the post-imperial period. At the royal monastery of Toling, one of the religious establishments newly founded in Gugé's domains, a translation academy was created, where Indian Buddhist scholars joined Rinchen Zangpo and his disciples. Tibetan translations, particularly of tantric materials, produced henceforth became known as the "new translations" (*sargyur*) in contradistinction to the "former translations" (*ngagyur*) of the Nyingmapa, whose tantric texts some believed to be apocryphal or corrupt.

29

After the royal monk Yeshé-ö's death, his successor Jangchub-ö continued his religious policies and in 1042 invited the Bengali scholar and adept Dīpaṃkaraśrījñāna, better known as Atiśa, from the great monastic university of Vikramaśīla in northeastern India to Gugé. After three years in residence there, during which he composed his famous *Lamp for the Path to Enlightenment* (Skt. *Bodhipathapradīpa*) on Mahāyāna practice, Atiśa traveled to Central Tibet, augmenting his Tibetan following until his death at Nyetang, near Lhasa, in 1054.

Atiśa appears in Tibetan accounts as an enthusiastic, generous, and saintly teacher, austere but also good natured, learned but more interested in the quality of practice than in scholarship per se. His successors, above all those in the lineage of his lay disciple Dromtön Gyelwé Jungné (1004–64), were known as Kadampa, "adherents of the scriptures and precepts," the first distinctively named Tibetan Buddhist order. Dromtön founded his seat at the monastery of Radreng ("Reting" in many Western sources), north of Lhasa, in 1057. The Kadampa are remembered for their concern for moral rigor in the pursuit of the bodhisattva's path, sometimes even emphasizing spiritual cultivation to the exclusion of the pursuit of learning. Nonetheless, Atiśa's own scholarly proclivities meant that some successors devoted themselves to study, so that the Kadampa became equally associated with philosophical education, above all at Sangpu, founded in 1071 by Atiśa's pupil Ngok Lekpé Sherap. The latter's nephew, Ngok Loden Sherap (1059–1109), who spent years studying in Kashmir and at Vikramaśīla itself, established a college there, whose traditions of logic and commentary formed the model for all later Tibetan monastic schools.

Owing to Atiśa's association with the Gugé kings, who were critical of the moral excesses attributed to some adherents of the tantras, and owing to certain cautions expressed in Atiśa's own writings, the Kadampa are sometimes regarded as a non-tantric lineage of Tibetan Buddhism. Atiśa himself, however, was a tantric adept and, despite the concerns expressed by some Tibetan disciples, he did teach aspects of tantrism in Tibet. His role in the promotion of the tantric cults of bodhisattva Avalokiteśvara and goddess Tārā was particularly great, and he was widely associated with the teaching of the *Guhyasamājatantra*, the "Esoteric Communion," one of the foremost Indian tantras. Nevertheless, the characteristic emphasis of his teaching was on the fundamental Mahāyāna doctrine of "emptiness imbued with compassion" (Skt. *śunyatā karuṇāgarbhā*), his insistence on which permeated all subsequent Tibetan Buddhist traditions. Atiśa's Kadampa successors created a remarkable corpus of literature devoted to this, called "training (or purification) of the mind (*lojong*)," in which everyday activities serve as focal points for the cultivation of spiritual love and a keen sense of the relativity of transient things.

The multiplication of lineages

Eleventh- and twelfth-century Buddhist revival saw intermittent tensions due to various factors: competing lines of transmission, regional and clan affiliations, relations between preexisting religious traditions and newly imported Indian teachings, orientations favoring monastic scholarship versus tantrism and yoga, and competition for patronage among them. It was in this setting that the guru, "lama" in Tibetan, became a focal point of religious and political authority. Though non-Tibetans often use the word *lama* to refer to Tibetan monks in general, it is a term that for Tibetans always retains a unique reference to the religious teacher who guides the spiritual life of the individual and of the community. One's lama is the revered authority to whom one owes absolute faith and loyalty, nothing less.

Despite the reticence of some toward aspects of tantrism, particularly ritualized sex and violence (whether these were actually practiced or, as was doubtlessly the usual case, merely symbolized), it was during this same period that efforts to translate and transmit tantric traditions were renewed. The new tantras reflected important changes within Indian Buddhist tantrism itself: roughly, a shift to systems emphasizing internal yoga over external ritual, the new systems being often transgressive and strongly eroticized in their symbolism and sometimes in fact. Indian tantric adepts claimed to possess particularly efficacious means to attain diverse spiritual powers, culminating in the highest enlightenment. The Tibetan masters following them sought to perpetuate such esoteric knowledge in Tibet, thereby asserting new sources of power, authority, and prestige.

Even though the age of the new tantric translations begins with Rinchen Zangpo, one of his junior contemporaries is counted among the first great proponents of these innovative forms of Indian Buddhist tantrism. Drokmi Śākya Yeshé (ca. 992–1064) was, like most who entered the saṅgha during his time, ordained within communities stemming from the tenth century monastic revival. After years of study in Nepal and India, he established his own monastic center and translation academy at Nyugulung, where he collaborated with the Indian tantric master Gayādhara. His most renowned contribution was the transmission of a tantric system called *Lamdré* ("Path and Fruit"), which came to be the central esoteric tradition of the Sakyapa order, whose chief monastery was founded by Könchok Gyelpo (1034–1102) of the aristocratic Khön household in 1071 or 1073. The *Lamdré*, based on the teachings of the important tantra dedicated to the divinity Hevajra, embraced both the "causal" teaching of the exoteric Mahāyāna and the "fruitional" instructions of the tantras. The first was summarized in terms of "three visions": the "impure vision" of ordinary beings; the "pure-and-impure vision" of bodhisattvas who are progressing on the Mahāyāna path; and the "pure vision" that characterizes the awakening of the buddhas. The tantras were similarly presented in three major topics, designated the "three continuums" (the word for "continuum" being, in fact, *tantra*, or *gyü* in Tibetan): (1) the continuum of the ground, the nature of reality in virtue of which awakening is possible; (2) the continuum of the path, namely, the stages of tantric practice; and (3) the continuum of the result, or fruit, in which the buddhahood that is latent in all reality is fully disclosed. The *Lamdré* has remained the preeminent system of spiritual instruction in the Sakyapa order down to the present time.

The Khön family produced a succession of influential masters in the following generations, especially those called the "five forebears" (Gongma-nga), of whom the first, Sachen Kunga Nyingpo (1092–1158), Könchok Gyelpo's son, contributed to shaping the early Sakya tradition as one of aristocratic patrons of Buddhism, committed to scholarly refinement while maintaining a specialized command of the ritual techniques of tantrism. One of Drokmi's chief successors, Zhangtön Chöbar, was Sachen's tutor, nurturing his charge to become the preeminent exponent of the *Lamdré* teaching. And two of Sachen's sons, Sonam Tsemo (1142–82) and Drakpa Gyeltsen (1147–1216), the second and third of the "five forebears," followed their father in remaining laymen and dedicated themselves exclusively to the family's religious and ritual tradition, becoming prolific teachers and authors.

Drokmi's many students included Marpa Chökyi Lodrö (ca. 1002–81), who was sent to study translation as a youth when his parents found him impossible to control. Eventually he rebelled against his teacher's exactions, for Drokmi's tutelage was not cheap, and set out on his own among the celebrated masters of India. Becoming famed as the leading Tibetan successor of the Indian adepts Nāropa and Maitripa, he attracted many followers, who, with their successors, came to be known as Kagyüpa, "adherents of the oral lineage." Just as Drokmi's lineage specialized in the system of the *Lamdré*, so Marpa's emphasized the paired systems of the "Six Teachings of Nāropa" and the Mahāmudrā, or "Great Seal." The first comprised the internal yogas of the highest tantras: Inner Heat, focusing upon the subtle energies of the body; the Body of Apparition, disclosing the illusory nature of appearances; the Dream, refining techniques of lucid dreaming (that is, dreaming while conscious that one is dreaming); and Luminosity, revealing reality to be radiant light. These four were methods for achieving liberation during this lifetime. The two remaining instructions concerned liberation at death: *powa*, the "transference" of consciousness, seeks to project the consciousness of one in the throes of death directly to a pure realm in which freedom is quickly gained; and *bardo*, the "intermediate state" between death and rebirth, guides one from infernal rebirth toward the achievement of freedom or felicity during the bewildering postmortem passage.

The second teaching with which Marpa is most often associated, that of the Mahāmudrā, addresses itself directly to the contemplative realization of the ultimate reality of mind, considered here as the "seal" stamped upon all possible modes of experience, both mundane and transcendent. The teaching has pronounced affinities with that of the Great Perfection tradition of the Nyingmapa, and later masters in both the Kagyüpa and Nyingmapa orders did not hesitate to propound an eclectic blend of both systems.

Marpa's best known disciple was Milarepa (1040–1123), the great Tibetan mystical poet, whose disciple Gampopa (1079–1153) established the Kagyüpa as a monastic tradition and sought to harmonize Marpa's esoteric teachings with the ethical instructions of the Kadampa, thus "mingling the two streams." Several of the Kagyüpa monastic orders that arose among his followers became major forces in later Tibetan religious and political life. Prominent among them were the "four senior Kagyü orders," originating with Gampopa's direct disciples. One of them, Pakmodrupa Dorjé Gyelpo (1110–70), in his turn gave rise to eight "junior" orders, established by his pupils. ("Junior" and "senior" designate only generational distance from Gampopa, not the relative importance of these orders.)

Notable among the four "senior" orders was that of the Karmapa, whose first representative was Düsum Khyenpa (1110–93). The eight "junior" orders prominently included the Drigungpa, following the brilliant and charismatic Drigung Kyobpa Jiktensumgön (1143–1217), and the Lingjé Kagyü of Lingjé Repa Pemadorjé (1128–88). It was a disciple of the latter, Tsangpa Gyaré (1161–1211), who established the Drukpa Kagyü order, which in the seventeenth century became the state religion of Bhutan, a nation whose proper name, Drukyül, the "Dragon Land," is in fact derived from that of its preeminent religious order.

Other important tantric lineages also arose during the same period, including those specializing in the *Tantra of the Wheel of Time* (*Kālacakratantra*), whose intricate system embraces not only yoga and ritual but also astronomical calculations, astrology, and medicine. The Jonangpa order, which was first established in western Tibet, was principally devoted to these instructions. In addition, the Shangpa Kagyü, founded by the enigmatic adept Khyungpo Neljor (ca. 1050–1140), emphasized techniques of lucid dreaming and teachings relating to the illusory quality of existence, while the lineage of "Pacification" (*Zhijé*), promulgated by the Indian teacher Padampa Sanggyé ("Holy Father Buddha," d. 1117), stressed the application of tantric practices to the realization of the central tenet of Mahāyāna Buddhism, the Perfection of Wisdom (Skt. Prajñāpāramitā). Padampa's most celebrated successor was a remarkable woman, Machik Lapdrön (ca. 1055–1143), whose special teaching, called the "Object of Severance" (*Chöyül*), dramatizes the adept's imagined self-sacrifice on behalf of all living beings. Its practice is accompanied by liturgies chanted to hauntingly beautiful melodies, exemplifying the frequent congruence in Tibet between tantric ritual and performance art. Machik's special teaching is preserved today in most orders of Tibetan Buddhism.

Later developments

In 1204, Śākyaśrībhadra, a respected teacher from Kashmir, arrived in Tibet with a retinue of Indian scholars, inspiring renewed enthusiasm for Indian learning. Künga Gyeltsen

(1182–1251) of Sakya, the fourth of the "five forebears" and later famed as "Sakya Paṇḍita," was among the young Tibetans who devoted themselves to the advancement of Indian intellectual traditions. Soon thereafter, the Mongol conquests, which had begun with the rise of Chinggis Khan (1167?–1227) and engulfed much of Asia and Eastern Europe, encroached upon Tibet. Prophecies appeared presaging a Mongol invasion, and these were realized in 1239 when the army of Dorta the Black arrived and ransacked the Kadampa temple of Radreng. The Mongols, however, withdrew without consolidating their rule in Tibet. In 1244 Sakya Paṇḍita embarked on a mission to the Mongol ruler, Godan Khan, arriving in 1246 and remaining among the Mongols until his death. His nephew Pakpa (1235–80), the last of the "five forebears," would later become the religious preceptor of Khubilai Khan, who honored him with the title "National Teacher" (*guoshi* in Chinese). In 1264 he was granted both religious and secular authority in Tibet, establishing a Sakyapa hegemony with Mongol backing, which would last for almost a century.

Members of non-Sakyapa orders also maintained relations with the Mongol lords, among them the second Karmapa hierarch, Karma Pakshi (1206–83), and his successor, Karmapa III Rangjung Dorjé (1284–1339). The Karmapas, who headed one of the prominent Kagyüpa orders, were instrumental in creating Tibet's unique form of ecclesiastical succession, in which a child is identified as the reborn emanation (*trülku*) and heir of a deceased master. The practice seems to have been first formalized when the infant Rangjung Dorjé was recognized as Karma Pakshi's immediate successor by one of the latter's foremost disciples, Orgyenpa (1230–1309). The period of Mongol-Sakyapa hegemony, enriched by the lavish patronage the Tibetan religious leadership received from the Mongol khans, also witnessed exceptional achievements in Tibetan Buddhist philosophy and art. The scholars Chomden Rikrel (1237–1305) and Butön Rinchendrup (1290–1364) catalogued and codified the massive Tibetan canons of Indian Buddhist scriptures and commentaries.

Trülku, the institution of the "reincarnated lama"

Following Orgyenpa's recognition of Rangjung Dorjé as the third Karmapa, the custom of identifying an infant as the rebirth of a leading hierarch and educating him to assume his predecessor's title and functions was widely adopted by monastic communities. The term for the Buddha's "body of emanation," *trülku* (Skt. *nirmāṇakāya*), became the designation for such identified rebirths, who were considered the emanations of buddhas or bodhisattvas. The custom permitted the monasteries to wrest a measure of freedom from the powerful families that were their patrons, for the *trülku* might be found among families of any social class and from any region. With the rise of the Dalai Lamas, the institution of the *trülku* had its greatest success, transforming Tibet into an ecclesiastical state.

At the same time, innovative (though sometimes controversial) philosophical systems were proposed by visionary teachers such as Dölpopa (1292–1361) of the Jonangpa order, who notably taught ultimate reality to be characterized as "extrinsic emptiness" (*zhentong*), and the Nyingmapa master Longchen Rapjampa (1308–63), a prolific exponent of the Great Perfection system of contemplation.

Toward 1350, under the leadership of Tai Situ Jangchup Gyeltsen (1302–64) of the Pakmodrupa, one of the four senior Kagyü orders, Tibet was freed from Sakyapa-Mongol rule. It was under the ensuing Pakmodrupa regime that Jé Tsongkhapa Lozang Drakpa (1357–1419) founded the Ganden monastery to the east of Lhasa (1409), soon to be the main seat of a new order, later known as Gelukpa, the "adherents of virtue." Tsongkhapa, a native of Amdo in the northeast who had come to Central Tibet as a teenager in order study with the well-known teachers of his day, was greatly revered for his vast learning and rigorous standards of practice. He became a prolific author, whose innovative interpretations sometimes challenged received opinion. His best-known work, the *Great Progression of the Path* (*Lamrim chenmo*), offers a massive and beautifully composed exposition of Atiśa's much admired *Lamp on the Path of Enlightenment*. A cultural innovator as well, Tsongkhapa established, also in 1409, the Great Prayer Festival marking the Tibetan New Year (usually in February) in Lhasa. The festival reasserted the centrality of Lhasa and its principal shrine, the seventh-century Jokhang Temple housing the ancient image of the Buddha said to have been brought to Tibet by the princess Wencheng, and was accompanied by pageantry recalling the epoch of Songtsen Gampo. Nevertheless, despite his great learning and sanctity, relations between his disciples and representatives of the older orders grew increasingly contentious following his death. The fifteenth and sixteenth centuries witnessed intensive doctrinal debate and political confrontation between the Gelukpa and their Sakyapa and Kagyüpa rivals.

Eight lineages, four orders

The major teaching traditions of Tibetan Buddhism are sometimes considered to form eight distinct lines of transmission, or lineages, passed down from master to disciple:

1. The *Nyingma*, or "Ancient Translation Tradition," derived from the teachings of Padmasambhava, Vimalamitra, and other eighth-century figures.
2. The *Kadam*, or "Tradition of Transmitted Precepts and Instructions," is traced to Atiśa and his Tibetan disciples, notably Dromtön.
3. *Lamdré*, the "Path with its Fruit," stems from the precepts of the Indian adept Virūpa, introduced into Tibet by the translator Drokmi.
4. The *Marpa Kagyü*, or "Oral Succession of Marpa," originates with the instructions of the Indian masters Tilopa, Nāropa, and Maitrīpa as transmitted to Marpa Chökyi Lodrö.

5. The *Shangpa Kagyü*, the "Oral Succession of Shangs Valley," is traced to Khyungpo Neljor, whose foremost teacher was the *ḍākinī* Niguma, said to have been the sister or wife of Nāropa.

6. The closely related teachings of *Zhijé*, "Pacification," and *Chöyül*, "Object of Severance," originated respectively with the Indian yogin Padampa Sanggyé and his Tibetan disciple, the yoginī Machik Lapdrön.

7. *Dorjé neljor*, the "Yoga of Indestructible Reality," is the system of yoga of the *Kālacakra Tantra*, as transmitted by the translator Gyijo Dawé Özer and others during the eleventh century.

8. *Dorjé-sum-gyi nyendrup*, the "Service and Attainment of the Three Adamant Realities," is a rare tradition derived from the goddess Vajrayoginī, as received by the Tibetan adept Orgyenpa in northwestern India.

The first four correspond to the major monastic orders: Nyingmapa, Gelukpa (which superseded the older Kadampa order), Sakyapa, and Kagyüpa. The Jonangpa order, surviving today in parts of Amdo, bases its teachings on the seventh lineage, that of the *Kālacakra Tantra*, and regards itself as a fifth monastic order, though this was not recognized under the traditional Tibetan government.

Although the four orders are thus closely related with major lineages, the two categories often intersect. Teachings originating in any of the eight lineages may in fact be transmitted in any of the four or five orders. Minor traditions exist, too, which do not fit clearly into these categories.

The connection between Tibetan Buddhism and imperial China forged under China's Mongol rulers did not come to an end after the Yuan dynasty fell in 1368. The close relationship between the Ming emperor Yongle (r. 1403–24) and the fifth Karmapa Dezhinshekpa (1384–1415) exemplifies this, and the Ming dynasty is often regarded as a period of Karmapa dominance in Sino-Tibetan affairs. Nonetheless, the Ming emperors refrained from favoring any single Tibetan school. Tsongkhapa's disciple, Jamchen Chöjé (1352–1435), who would establish Sera Monastery near Lhasa in 1419, among others, also received imperial honors at the Chinese court. Although formal ties between China's rulers and Tibetan religious leaders continued under the Ming, it is important to note that China exercised no political authority in Tibet at this time, and that, besides trade, Sino-Tibetan relations during this period remained largely ceremonial and symbolic.

Tsongkhapa's successors established new monasteries throughout Tibet, gathering the support of leading princes and powerful families. Gendün-drup (1391–1474), for instance, founded the Trashi Lhünpo monastery in Tsang. He and his successor, Gendün Gyatso (1476–1542), were primarily remembered for their scholarly and spiritual attainments, and under their guidance Trashi Lhünpo became one of the preeminent Gelukpa centers, the base for the order's expansion in western Tibet. Their success would have significant political repercussions during the following centuries, when the rulers of Tsang came to favor the Gelukpa's rivals, the Karmapas, above all. Gendün Gyatso, in all events, left Trashi Lhünpo early in his teaching career, taking up a new position at Drepung monastery, which had been founded by Tsongkhapa's disciple Jamyang Chöjé in 1416 on the outskirts of Lhasa.

By the sixteenth century, major powers in Central Tibet were allied with the Gelukpa, while the kings of Tsang supported the Kagyüpa, Jonangpa and other orders. Gendün Gyatso's successor, Sonam Gyatso (1543–88), embarked on missionary work among the Mongols, and, on winning the allegiance of the Tümed chieftain Altan Khan (1578), received the Mongolian title Dalai Lama ("oceanic guru"). Because this title was bestowed posthumously on his predecessors, he became the third in the

4. The fifteenth-century monastery of Tiksé in Ladakh illustrates the rapid spread of the Gelukpa order in far western Tibet. Its fortress-like architecture, dominating a hilltop, is typical of many Tibetan administrative and religious establishments, notably the Potala in Lhasa.

line. The connection he forged with the Mongols encouraged the renewed interest of the Mongolian leadership in Tibetan affairs and, after his passing, his successor, the fourth Dalai Lama Yönten Gyatso (1589–1617), was recognized among the Mongol aristocracy. In 1642 Gushri Khan of the Khoshud tribe conquered all of Tibet, establishing the fifth Dalai Lama Ngawang Gyatso (1617–82) as titular ruler of the reunified realm. The kingdom of Tsang was suppressed, together with the religious traditions it had favored, above all the Jonangpa, who were banned from all but a few Tibetan territories outside the sphere of the Dalai Lama's control. The government of the "Great Fifth," as he became known to posterity, adopted a policy of mass monasticism in all parts of the country and new Gelukpa establishments were founded everywhere, while many centers of the older orders and of the Bön religion were now required to embrace the Gelukpa tradition as well.

The Tibetan political system, in the form in which it was developed
by the fifth Dalai Lama and his successors, valorized the ideal
of an equilibrium between the religious and secular branches
of government (*chösi nyiden*), though in fact the ecclesiastical
offices came to dominate Tibetan administration. The Great
Fifth's regime, known after the name of his residence at Drepung
Monastery as the Ganden Podrang ("Tuṣita Palace"), marked its
presence in Lhasa with the construction of the soaring Potala
Palace atop "Red Hill" (Marpori) in the southern quarter of the
town. The fifth Dalai Lama also elevated the status of his tutor, the
learned lama Lozang Chögyen (1567–1662), who was granted the
title of Panchen Lama. He was regarded as either first or fourth
in the line depending on whether his supposed predecessors
were counted, beginning with Tsongkhapa's illustrious disciple
Khedrup-jé (1385–1438). The seat of the Panchen Lamas was
established at Trashi Lhünpo, where their authority sometimes
rivaled that of the Dalai Lamas themselves.

The fifth Dalai Lama visited the court in Beijing soon after the
inception of the Qing dynasty (1644–1911) under China's Manchu
conquerors. During the decades that followed, Tibet increasingly
emerged as a focal point of competition between Manchus and
Mongols in their rivalry for hegemony in Central Asia. The
controversial sixth Dalai Lama, Tsangyang Gyatso (1683–1706), a
libertine who preferred wine and women to the life of a monk, was
forcibly removed from office by Tibet's Mongol overlord Lhazang
Khan and died under mysterious circumstances while en route to
the Chinese capital. In 1717 the Zunghar Mongols invaded Tibet,
bringing renewed civil war and intersectarian violence. During
the 1720s the Manchus, campaigning against the Zunghars and
Tibetan factions allied with them, sought to consolidate their
rule over large parts of the eastern Tibetan provinces of Amdo
and Kham. Leading Gelukpa hierarchs from Amdo, such as the
Qianlong emperor's teacher Changkya Rölpé Dorjé (1717–86),
came to play important roles in the religious affairs of the Manchu
empire.

The intermittent struggles in Central Tibet throughout the seventeenth and eighteenth centuries helped to transform Tibet's religious geography more generally. For centuries Central Tibet had been the clear center of gravity in Tibetan spiritual life, but masters of eastern Tibetan origin, and sometimes others as well, now began to focus their efforts increasingly in far eastern Kham and Amdo. This had many causes and consequences. A case in point may be seen in the career of the Tenth Karmapa, Chöying Dorjé (1605–74), an artist of considerable genius. Crowned during his youth as "king of Tibet" by the rulers of Tsang, he was forced into exile with the ascent of the fifth Dalai Lama and passed much of his life in the far southeast of Tibet, in what is today Yunnan, where he was honored by the rulers of the Naxi Kingdom based in Lijiang.

In Kham, moreover, with the support of the rulers of the Dergé principality, eastern Tibetan Karmapa and Sakyapa masters contributed to the creation of Tibet's greatest publishing house, the Dergé Printery, whose eighteenth-century edition of the Tibetan Buddhist canon is considered to be among the greatest achievements of traditional Tibetan printing. During this period, too, several of the Gelukpa monasteries of eastern Tibet, such as Kumbum, near Tsongkhapa's birthplace not far from the city of Xining (Qinghai Province), and Labrang Trashi-khyil, founded by Jamyang Zhepa (1648–1721) in southern Gansu, also began to achieve prominence in arts and learning. Scholars associated with these latter centers were often not ethnic Tibetans, and they frequently enjoyed the patronage of the Manchu court, which regarded Tibetan Buddhism as supplying a common cultural milieu for the peoples of Inner Asia.

Nineteenth-century Kham became home to a dynamic movement often characterized as "eclectic" or "nonpartisan" (*rimé*), which sought to defuse the intense sectarianism that had plagued Tibetan Buddhism. The encyclopedic writings of Jamyang Khyentsé Wangpo (1810–92) and Jamgön Kongtrül (1813–99) became virtually a new canon for the adherents of this tolerant trend. One of their disciples, Mipam Namgyel (1846–1912) also elaborated a revised scholastic curriculum emphasizing the doctrinal standpoint of the Nyingmapa order. Though the thirteenth Dalai Lama (1876–1933) was sympathetic to the broad orientations of these teachers, the Gelukpa hierarchy was generally more reserved. Indeed, one of the Dalai Lama's own tutors, Pabongkhapa Dechen Nyingpo (1878–1941), on the basis of his visions of the spirit Dorjé Shukden, became harshly critical of the other schools of Tibetan Buddhism and the Bön religion, provoking violent confrontations on several occasions. Sectarian tensions continued endemically throughout the twentieth century in Tibet and, after 1959, in exile as well.

Chapter 4
Spiritual exercise and the path of the bodhisattva

By the early second millennium, Buddhist teachings concerning the painful round of rebirth (*saṃsāra*) and the virtuous or evil deeds (*karman*) that condition rebirth within it, together with conceptions of the beatitude realized by those who, as Buddhas and bodhisattvas moved by compassion and wisdom, surpass mundane existence, had become widespread in Tibetan culture overall. Nevertheless, few Tibetans traditionally, even counting those who were monks or nuns, were beneficiaries of formal religious education beyond a rudimentary level. Their knowledge of merit and demerit, of the purification to be achieved and blessings to be gained through activities of worship and pilgrimage, of the necessity of maintaining devoted respect for the lamas and the divinities—this and much more was imbued by partaking of the daily life of the communities to which they belonged. In practices such as pilgrimage and the cults of widely worshipped divinities, such as Avalokiteśvara, the "Buddhist basics" were systematically reinforced. This may be seen in an elegy of worship performed at a pilgrimage site near the Nepal-Tibet border, which reads in part:

> All those who offer flowers here will obtain the perfect liberty and
>   endowment of human birth.
> All those who offer incense will attain pure moral discipline.
> All those who offer butter-lamps will be freed from the darkness of
>   unknowing.

Perhaps only a few Tibetans read such texts, but affirmations such as these formed part of common oral tradition.

Ordering time and space

Tibetan Buddhism, like other religions, structures society and the individual agent through the order it imposes upon space and time. This principle operates in the intimacy of the family home, with its domestic shrine and the regular cycle of religious activities in which household members engage, and on a national level in connection with Tibet's sacred geography and the major events marking its ritual calendar. Between these extremes, the spatial ordering of monastery, temple, and town, and the temporal ordering of observances within them exemplify Buddhism's role in forming Tibetan experiences and orientations.

In Tibetan societies, the deference of social inferior to superior, junior to senior, mundane to sacred, spiritually immature to spiritually advanced, and so forth is very strongly marked. A comportment of modesty and humility must be adopted when one enters a temple, greats a monk or, especially, a lama, and when one attends to the arrangement of the household shrine. Images of the buddhas and living teachers alike are honored with prostrations, and holy persons, places, and structures (such as temples and stūpas) are kept to one's right, so that, instead of seeking the shortest route between two points, one must adhere to a pattern of clockwise circumambulation. (In the case of the Bön religion, though, circumambulation is practiced in the opposite, counterclockwise direction.) Deference is additionally marked by donations and offerings, including incense and lamps (or butter to aliment them), flowers and foodstuff, cash and valuables, as well as the ubiquitous ceremonial scarves called *khatak*. The latter are classed by materials (gauze, linen, silk), design (plain or embroidered), size and color (usually white). To offer a *khatak* that fails to correspond to the status of the recipient may in certain contexts be regarded as a severe breach of manners.

The monastery or temple will typically contain a courtyard leading to the principle shrine, which is often placed within an assembly hall. It is here that the monks (or, in some cases, lay practitioners) gather as required by the regular ritual cycle, or for services necessitated by special circumstances (for instance, for funerals). In a village temple or before a household shrine, there may be room for only a few to assemble, while in larger monasteries the congregation may number several thousand, seated in strict accordance with rank and ritual order. Some of these protocols are based on stipulations found in the Vinaya, but above all on established customs within Tibetan monastic communities, as specified within the monastic charters (*chayik*).

Spatial order is complemented by the rhythms punctuating day, month, and year. At dawn, after rising, one tends to the

5. At this assembly, the ranking *trülku*, wearing the pointed "paṇḍita" hat, sits in the *center*, the ritual master, wearing the "lotus" hat, to his *left*. The remaining monks, all attired similarly, are seated in order of rank.

arrangement of the altar, replenishing the seven bowls of water that symbolize offerings of drinking water, bathing water, flowers, incense, lamps, perfumes, and nourishment, the gifts appropriate for an honored guest according to Indian Buddhist traditions. A compassionate offering of consecrated water may then be dedicated to the *yidak* (Skt. *preta*), the "hungry ghosts" who are incapable of absorbing other nutrition. When the morning tea is served, whether in a lay home, a monk's personal residence, or in the assembly, a prayer service must first be offered. Even those without formal religious training usually know the basic formulas recited before tea or meals:

> The supreme teacher is the precious Buddha;
> The supreme protector is the precious Dharma;
> The supreme guide is the precious Saṅgha—
> I offer worship to these Three Refuge-granting Jewels!

At dusk, a service is dedicated to the "lords" (*gönpo*), the wrathful protective divinities. As the day draws to an end, the altar is cleansed, the water bowls emptied, and one prepares for sleep with prayers.

The monthly cycle, which follows the lunar calendar, places particular emphasis on the new and full moon days, which are considered favorable times for rites of purification, sometimes accompanied by a partial fast. For practitioners of tantric ritual, the tenth day of the month is the feast day of the Guru, while the twenty-fifth is consecrated to the *ḍākinī*, the goddess embodying enlightened wisdom.

The year, too, is punctuated by regular observances, beginning with the festivities of the new year (*losar*) and concluding with offerings to the protective divinities to purge the year's accumulated evils and sins. In between, dates held sacred throughout Tibet include the full moon of the fourth month (*Saga* in Tibetan, *Vesakh* in Pali), which is the day of the Buddha's enlightenment and final passing; the "general fumigation of the world" (*dzamling chisang*) in the fifth month; and the twenty-second of the ninth month, commemorating the Buddha's descent to the island of Laṅkā following his visit to his deceased mother in the heavens. Many festivals and holidays relate to specific locations, temples, or religious orders. Examples include the twenty-seventh of the twelfth month, when the blessing of the sacred ceremonial dagger (*purba*) of Sera monastery is publicly granted, or the fourteenth of the eleventh month, observed in the Sakyapa order as the death anniversary of Sakya Paṇḍita.

Many important pilgrimages and festivals, moreover, may be determined by the twelve-year animal cycle of Chinese origin. Thus, the sacred mountain of west Tibet, Kailash (Tib. *Gang Rinpoché*), is a focal point for pilgrimage in the horse year, and the Pure Crystal Mountain of Tsari, in southeastern Tibet, in the monkey year. The great teaching of the "tranference of consciousness" (*powa*) at Drigung monastery is also conferred in the monkey year.

The general patterns described here were mostly well established early in the early second millennium, when the major orders were formed. Then, as now, the teachings and practices of Tibetan Buddhists did not occur on a neutral, empty stage but unfolded in a domain of structured space and time, in which body, speech, and mind must conform with principles of hierarchy, deference, and personal modesty. It is upon these foundations that the elaborate educational, ritual, and contemplative constructions of the tradition were raised.

The message of the Kadampa

Tradition recalls the period following the collapse of the Tibetan empire as a dark age, when Buddhism was suppressed, and learning and letters were no more. Translation activity and the scholarship associated with it were severely reduced until the end of tenth century, when the West Tibetan kingdom of Gugé began to patronize Buddhist art and learning once again. Henceforth, conditions favoring doctrinal and philosophical investigations reemerged.

Paradigmatic of this revival was the long, influential sojourn of the Bengali scholar and saint Atiśa, first in Gugé (1042–45) and then in Central Tibet until his death in 1054. Atiśa sought to emphasize above all the ethical grounding of Mahāyāna Buddhism, and his teachings became the basis for subsequent Tibetan education concerning the Mahāyāna path. Atiśa's essential framework for instruction here was a moral theory that recognized three grades of aspirant, as defined in his widely read *Lamp on the Path of Enlightenment (Bodhipathapradīpa)*:

> Whoever by whatever means strives for his own sake
> Only for saṃsāra's pleasures—that one is the *lesser person*.
> Turning his back to worldly pleasure, and shunning sinful deeds,
> The soul who strives for his own peace is called the *middling person*.
> One who, owing to the pain of his own existence, wholeheartedly
>   seeks to end
> All the pain of others—that is the *superior person*.

As we are all, to whatever extent, self-interested, we inevitably partake of the character of "lesser" and "middling" persons, to whom the fundamental teachings on the impermanence and suffering of the world in general are addressed. However, Atiśa's overriding concern was to encourage the practice of "superior persons," beginning with the cultivation of the "enlightened spirit" (*bodhicitta*) of the bodhisattva:

> Regarding all sentient beings,
> And beginning with a loving mind,
> You consider creatures without exception,
> Like those born in the three lower destinies [of hells, ghosts, and
>   animals],
> And those pained by death and transference [to a new birth].
> Then you generate the enlightened spirit

With an irreversible vow,
Desiring to liberate suffering beings
From pain and the causes of pain.

Atiśa's approach to the gradual path of the Mahāyāna, beginning
with aspiration for enlightenment and culminating in the realization
of emptiness, inspired all Tibetan Buddhist traditions. Particularly
influential elaborations include *The Jewel Ornament of Liberation*
by the founder of the Kagyü monastic orders, Gampopa, and *The
Great Progression of the Path*, the masterwork of Jé Tsongkhapa. The
key teachings contained in these works are sometimes summarized
as the "four reversals of attitude" (*lodok namzhi*):

1. to reverse clinging to the pleasures of this life, one
    contemplates this "precious human birth" and its
    impermanence, the inevitability of death;
2. to reverse clinging to the idea of favorable rebirth as an
    appropriate goal, one contemplates the ubiquitous suffering of
    saṃsāra and the causal operations of karma, the positive and
    negative deeds driving rebirth;
3. to reverse striving for personal liberation as one's aim,
    one cultivates, with loving kindness and compassion, the
    enlightened spirit (*jangchup-sem*, Skt. *bodhicitta*) so as to
    achieve enlightenment for all beings;
4. to reverse clinging to ephemeral things as ultimately real,
    one contemplates the emptiness (*tongpanyi*, Skt. *śūnyatā*) of
    conditioned existence, the illusion-like nature of appearances.

One whose spiritual outlook is determined by the vow of the
bodhisattva is committed to accumulating the dual provisions
of merit and wisdom by cultivating the six perfections of the
bodhisattva's path: generosity, moral discipline, forbearance, effort,
meditation, and wisdom. The virtues of the bodhisattva were
extolled at length in the half-dozen Indian works that came to be
known in Tibet as the "six texts of the Kadam order," the principal
texts studied among the first generations of Atiśa's disciples. These

six books are often described as forming three pairs: the first two, the *Udānavarga* ("Collection of Aphorisms") and *Jātakamālā* ("Garland of Birth-Tales"), are edifying works, containing verses and stories exemplifying the ideals of the Buddhist life, and the self-sacrifice and endurance of the bodhisattva as he progresses through diverse lifetimes toward perfection. The second pair, the *Śikṣāsamuccaya* ("Compendium of Lessons") and *Bodhicaryāvatāra* ("Introduction to Enlightened Conduct"), both attributed to the eighth-century master Śāntideva, emphasizes practical guidance on the Mahāyāna path in its ethical dimensions. The last pair, the *Mahāyānasūtrālaṃkāra* ("Ornament of the Mahāyāna Sūtras") and *Bodhisattvabhūmi* ("Bodhisattva Stage"), elaborates the same path from a preeminently doctrinal and theoretical perspective.

Corresponding to the Kadampa textual curriculum, and relating with particular clarity to the two works of Śāntideva on the practice of the path, is the genre of *lojong*, "mind-training," or "spiritual

The progressive path to enlightenment

The Mahāyāna "progressive path of enlightenment" (*jangchup lamrim*) was understood similarly in all the Tibetan Buddhist orders. Its major themes, with minor modifications in the various traditions, were often outlined as follows:

Introductory

1. The merits of the teacher and the qualities to be cultivated by the pupil

I. Path of the "lesser person"

2. Understanding the precious opportunity afforded by human birth
3. Contemplation of death and impermanence

II. Path of the "middling person"

4. Contemplation of karma, the principle of the impersonal operations of moral causation
5. Contemplation of the sufferings of beings in saṃsāra, from those in the lowest realms to the worldly gods
6. Understanding the benefits of liberation, and seeking refuge in the Three Jewels of Buddha, Dharma, and Saṅgha

III. Path of the "superior person"

7. Cultivation of the "four immeasurables": compassion, loving kindness, sympathetic joy and equanimity on behalf of all beings
8. The vow of the bodhisattva, to achieve enlightenment on behalf of all living beings
9–12. The actual practice of the bodhisattva (i.e., the six transcendent perfections, of which the first four are generosity, ethical discipline, patience, and constant effort)
13. The fifth perfection, absorption in meditation, identified as the cultivation of tranquility (Skt. *śamatha*, Tib. *zhiné*)
14. The sixth perfection, wisdom (Skt. *prajñā*, Tib. *sherap*), the cultivation of contemplative insight (Skt. *vipaśyanā*, Tib. *lhaktong*), whereby emptiness comes to be directly realized
15. Introduction to the special teachings of the tantras

Additional topics that may be introduced in manuals on the path include the formal analysis of the "stages and paths" (Tib. *salam*) traversed by the bodhisattva, and the qualities of the enlightened buddhas, in particular, their embodiments (Skt. *kāya*, Tib. *ku*), gnosis (Skt. *jñāna*, Tib. *yeshé*), and activities on behalf of beings (Skt. *buddhakarma*, Tib. *sanggyé trinlé*).

exercise." *Lojong* is concerned with the practical challenges of the Mahāyāna path, the need for constant training of thought, speech, and action in order to attune oneself to the ideal of a life wholly directed to the enlightenment of the Buddha. The practice focuses upon the active cultivation of equanimity, compassion, loving-kindness, and other virtues, together with an awareness of the world as fleeting and empty, but it also involves practical details of daily life: how to eat and to drink, what to think while falling asleep, passing in and out of doors, mounting the stairs, going to the toilet, etc. Thus *lojong*, together with the Indian works that inspired it, became part of the common heritage of Tibetan Buddhism, informing the ethical education of both monk and layperson. An example may be seen in a letter of spiritual advice addressed to a thirteenth-century Mongol noblewoman, in which Khubilai Khan's Tibetan preceptor, the lama Pakpa (1235–80), writes:

> When entering the road say, "May I enter enlightenment's path!"
> On crossing a river say, "May I traverse the torrent of sorrow!"
> When you climb up a stairway say, "May I ascend the stairway of freedom!"
> When meeting someone say, "May I meet with sublime individuals!"
> When you see an empty pot say, "May I be empty of faults!"
> When you see a full pot say, "May I be full of good qualities!"

Lojong, in short, constitutes the fabric upon which much of Tibetan Buddhist practice is arrayed, in virtue of which that practice is coherent and whole, and not merely an aggregation of doctrines, rituals, and routines. The compassionate outlook it seeks to reinforce is expressed in a broad range of Tibetan customs; a striking example is *tsetar*, the "freeing of life," whereby one ransoms an animal destined for slaughter so that it is free to live out its natural term. (It may be noted, however, that this custom concerns merit-making on behalf of the donor no less than mercy for the fate of the victim.)

One of the most popular disciplines of *lojong* is *tonglen*, literally, "sending and receiving." As in many forms of Buddhist meditation, the focal point here is the breath, the mindful attention to inhalations and exhalations while seated in the appropriate posture. But in *tonglen*, attention to the breath is accompanied by an elementary visualization exercise, in which you imagine all the sufferings of beings throughout the world taking the form of black smoke, which you absorb and dissolve with each inhalation. With each exhalation, you emit a radiant light characterized by the warmth of love, which touches all beings, healing their ills and granting them peace. Meditating in this way, you cultivate the understanding that self and other are ultimately no different and so realize that self and other may be exchanged. This training of compassion imbued with profound empathy should continue until other is valued above self.

The relativity of self and other in Mahāyāna thought pertains not only to the cultivation of benevolence but to the fundamental insight that all phenomena are conditioned and interdependent, and thus "empty" (Tib. *tongpa*, Skt. *śūnya*). This understanding is the hallmark of the sixth perfection of the bodhisattva, that of wisdom (Tib. *sherap*, Skt. *prajñā*), and was given its classical philosophical articulation by the second-century Indian teacher Nāgārjuna, whose tradition Atiśa upheld. He did not regard Nāgārjuna's thought to be captured by the strictures of philosophical argument alone but to be disclosed, rather, in the cultivation of contemplative insight. For Atiśa, meditation on emptiness was the essential practice and theoretical reason was of only limited value in this respect:

> [Investigations of] perception and inference are unnecessary.
> They have been formulated by the learned to refute the disputations
>   of non-Buddhists.

Nevertheless, he deemed the analysis of everyday phenomena to be the fundamental means to arrive at the insight that

> There is neither seeing nor seer, but peace without beginning or end . . .
> Neither an abode nor that which abides, no coming or going,
>   unexemplified,

Ineffable, not to be viewed, unchanging, uncompounded—
If the adept realizes just this, affective and cognitive obscurations
      are abandoned.

In brief, Atiśa, following Nāgārjuna's commentator Candrakīrti, held that although our everyday language adequately describes apparent reality, philosophical discourse nevertheless has a necessary role: not system-building but the criticism of our presuppositions, dismantling them until we arrive at the profound realization of emptiness and the opening that this entails.

Atiśa on the bodhisattva's path:

All doctrines of the path are included in the six transcendent perfections. If you realize emptiness without error, and are without desire, grasping, or attachment towards outer or inner entities, you are continually graced with the perfection of generosity. Because, without grasping or attachment, one is untainted by unvirtue, you are continually graced with the perfection of moral discipline. Because there is then no enmity due to clinging to I and mine, you are continually graced with the perfection of forebearance. Because the mind becomes enthusiastic after realizing that, you are continually graced with the perfection of effort. Because there is no distraction when entities are transcended, you continually are graced with the perfection of meditation. Because there is no intellectual engagement in the three spheres [of subject, object, and their interaction], you are continually graced with the transcendent perfection of wisdom.

from Chegom Dzongpa, *Scattered Sayings of the Kadampa Masters*

. . . and on the practice of "mind-training" (lojong):

All doubts are to be abandoned, and assiduousness in practice
    to be cherished.
Renouncing sleep, torpor and lassitude, I must always make
    energetic efforts.

> With mindfulness, attentiveness and care, thoroughly
>   guarding the senses,
> During three periods, day and night, I must examine the
>   stream of the mind.
> I am to proclaim my own faults, not look to those of others.
> I must conceal my excellences, while proclaiming those of
>   others. ...
> Dwelling in wilderness retreats, may I put myself into hiding,
> Like the dead corpse of a beast, and dwell there free from
>   desire. ...
> When among many, may I watch my speech.
> When alone, may I watch my mind!
>
> from Atiśa, *The Bodhisattva's Jeweled Necklace*

Avalokiteśvara: the bodhisattva of compassion

By adopting an enlightened spirit and vowing to act in accord with the path of the Mahāyāna, one becomes an aspiring bodhisattva. Those who make great progress on this path, and who, after many lifetimes of striving, attain direct insight into emptiness, come to realize the ten stages that define the higher reaches of that path, culminating in the achievement of a buddha's awakening. Several of the great human teachers, such as the Indian masters Nāgārjuna and Asaṅga, are supposed to have arrived at the first or even the third among the ten stages. But the highest stages, and particularly the tenth, just preceding buddhahood, are believed to be the domain of divine bodhisattvas, who subsist for many eons and embody precise facets of the Buddha's enlightenment. Thus, Mañjuśrī, often depicted as a sword-wielding youth, is the very incarnation of perfect insight, and Vajrapāṇi, the wrathful "bearer of the Vajra-scepter," is regarded as the apotheosis of spiritual power. Together with Avalokiteśvara, who is Supreme Compassion, these are the best known of the divine bodhisattvas and are often regarded as forming a trinity called the "Lords of the Three Clans." Typically, they were the patron-divinities of renowned teachers, who are sometimes also regarded as their emanations. Among the "five forebears" of the Sakyapa, for instance, Drakpa Gyeltsen is often thought to have embodied Vajrapāṇi, and Sakya Paṇḍita, Mañjuśrī. Jé Tsongkhapa, too, is identified with the bodhisattva of wisdom, while the Karmapas and the Dalai Lamas are thought to be Avalokiteśvara (Tib. *Chenrezi*). These and many other bodhisattvas are described in the teachings of the Mahāyāna sūtras, and their cults were further developed in the tantras as well. Avalokiteśvara, who was regarded as Tibet's divine protector overall, enjoying a special place in Tibetan historical and mythological conceptions, provides the clearest example of these developments.

Although Buddhist teachings relating to Avalokiteśvara had been introduced to Tibet by the eighth and ninth centuries, Atiśa played a cardinal role in promoting this bodhisattva among Tibetans from the eleventh century on. In the form in which he was usually represented by Atiśa, he was to be imagined as a white, four-armed figure, with two hands clasped as in prayer and holding a wishing gem, and the two to his sides holding, respectively, a rosary and a white lotus. His *mantra* is the six-syllable formula *Oṃ maṇipadme hūṃ*, an homage to the one "holding gem (*maṇi*) and lotus (*padma*)" and not meaning, as Western writers often suppose, "hail to the jewel in the lotus." (Tibetans, in any event, are seldom interested in the semantic meaning of this mantra and prefer to interpret its six syllables symbolically as conveying the blessings of compassion to beings inhabiting the six realms of worldly existence.) In this form, Avalokiteśvara is known as "Six Syllables."

Atiśa's teaching of Six Syllables corresponded to his emphasis on the teaching of compassion as the proper motivation for the Mahāyāna path. It was a teaching that was also tinged with elements of tantrism, in particular, in its use of visualization and mantra, and in its promulgation by means of a special initiation in which the disciple is granted the meditation instruction and mantra by a qualified preceptor. Though visualization exercises are found throughout Buddhist meditation teachings—we have seen this in the example of *tonglen*—tantric visualization is distinctive in that it often requires the meditator to identify herself with the deity contemplated. Atiśa's teaching of Avalokiteśvara directed Tibetans to find the bodhisattva of Supreme Compassion within themselves and in all others as well.

Such was his popularity that Six Syllables was retrojected into the Tibetan past, to become the progenitor of the Tibetan people. According to the popular myth, Avalokiteśvara, in the form of a divine monkey, coupled with an ogress (identified with goddess Tārā), and from their union the Tibetans were born. He was believed, too, to have appeared as the emperor Songtsen Gampo, whose promotion of the arts of civilization was regarded as the evidence of the bodhisattva's abiding compassion. In the twelfth century, the treasure-doctrines of the Nyingmapa tradition greatly amplified the growing mythology. In this revealed literature, Atiśa's ethically oriented doctrine merges with the Great Perfection teaching, with its emphasis on discovering ultimate reality in the dynamic flow of ordinary awareness.

The most famous of these new revelations was the corpus known as the *Maṇi Kabum*, the "Collected Works on Maṇi," *maṇi* designating the six-syllable mantra. These works are attributed to Songtsen Gampo, and in them we find a rich, legendary tapestry in which Songtsen Gampo, princess Wencheng, and others in the royal family and court figure as culture heroes, much as do Arthur, Guinevere, and the Knights of the Round Table in the medieval traditions of England and France. Supreme Compassion, the preferred name for Avalokiteśvara in these texts, is regarded as the basis for love, kindness, and nurturing among all creatures, but at

A meditation on Avalokiteśvara

When you cultivate the realization that your own mind is
 Supreme Compassion [enlightened qualities] arise by
 themselves.

Thus his body, which is free from birth and death, is like a
 reflected image: it is free, it appears, but it is devoid of
 substantial existence.

Speech as Supreme Compassion is like an echo, and is
 incessant.

Oṃ Maṇipadme Hūṃ, the natural voice of Reality, is
 uninterrupted:

Oṃ stills pride, purifies the heavens of the gods, and cuts off
 birth amongst them.

Ma stills jealous rage, purifies the realms of the demigods, and
 cuts off birth amongst them.

Ṇi stills lust, purifies the world of human beings, and cuts off
 birth amongst them.

Pad stills stupidity, purifies the habitats of animals, and cuts off
 birth amongst them.

Me stills greed, purifies the lands of tormented spirits, and cuts
 off birth amongst them.

Hūṃ stills hatred, purifies the hells, and cuts off birth within
 them.

from the *Maṇi Kabum*

the same time he is none other than the creative power of mind,
whose infinite potentialities for self-actualization constitute the
very basis for creation itself.

In the teaching of Avalokiteśvara, the "Buddhist basics" are
expressed in particularly Tibetan form. The lessons of the
Kadampa teachings of altruism and ethical excellence, seen
in Atiśa's insistence on the essence of Mahāyāna teaching as
"emptiness imbued with compassion," are seamlessly integrated

with elementary tantric practice, focusing on the visualization of the deity and the recitation of his mantra, and informed by the Great Perfection tradition's emphasis on finding enlightenment in the here and now. This defines a widespread cultural synthesis, serving to ground the concerns of the more specialized intellectual and ritual traditions of Tibetan Buddhism.

Chapter 5
Philosophical developments and disputes

Tibetan monastic education

Under the Tibetan empire, Buddhist monks performed secretarial and clerical duties for the state bureaucracy. This reflected the monasteries' capacity to provide a modicum of education including training in essential scribal skills. Learned monks also served as tutors to the Tibetan royal family. Nevertheless, monastic scholars did not entirely supplant the civil bureaucracy of the period, not to mention the military administration.

With the ninth-century collapse of the Tibetan empire, this picture changed. After the administration of the old Tibetan state declined, learning and literacy came to be preserved primarily among lay and monastic religious specialists. One mark of the religious domination of written Tibetan may be seen in the transformation of the language itself: the archaic language now referred to as "Old Tibetan" fell into disuse, and the originally artificial conventions of Buddhist scriptural translations became the model for what we know today as "Classical Tibetan." From the tenth century to recent times, formal education thus became primarily an aspect of religious training, the main exceptions being education within families practicing specialized vocations (such as art, medicine, and astrology) and aristocratic families, who nevertheless often continued the ancient tradition of inviting learned monks to serve as tutors. In communities with strong traditions of lay Buddhist devotion, even among nomads and peasants, basic literacy was sometimes also maintained.

The level of literacy, whether of monks, nuns, or laypersons, was frequently rudimentary. Recognition of the letters of the alphabet permitted one to use prayer books as memory aids for the devotions one practiced, but the mastery of the complex rules of Tibetan spelling and grammar, together with the fine calligraphic penmanship that was essential for all occupations requiring writing, were the domain of few people. This mastery was usually a prerequisite for advanced education of any kind, excepting those monks who were educated primarily through debate practice and who were sometimes not very well trained in writing.

In the monasteries, young novices were expected to memorize the texts recited as part of the ritual cycle of the monastery to which they belonged. Rote memorization, whether or not one understood the words, was key here. For a primary function of the monastery was to ensure the regular performance of rites deemed essential for magnifying the merits of donors and protecting the community, including rulers and subjects. Prominent among ritual texts were invocations of buddhas, bodhisattvas and the teachers of one's lineage; offerings to the many divinities of the Buddhist pantheon, as well as to the properly Tibetan protective deities; confessionals and purifications; dedications of the merits achieved through donation or religious practice; and much more. Monasteries typically required their monks to be familiar with hundreds of pages to secure the smooth performance of regular and punctual rituals. Before very recent times, for many, and perhaps most monks, formal education ended here.

Small numbers among the monastics, however, were motivated and encouraged to pursue higher levels of education. This often meant moving from one's home monastery to a larger center with better facilities, perhaps even a formally constituted college. It was not uncommon for monks seeking higher education to transfer their monastic residence in this way several times, until finding what they regarded as the most promising circumstances in which to pursue their studies, above all at the monastic colleges of the great Gelukpa monasteries of Central Tibet and Tsang—Ganden, Sera, Drepung, and Trashi Lhünpo. Those adhering to other orders gravitated to colleges affiliated with the traditions to which they belonged, though the predominance of the big Gelukpa institutions guaranteed that they drew their share of visiting students from these orders too.

From the late eleventh century on, the monastic colleges emphasized a highly rationalized approach to Buddhist doctrine. At the forefront of this development was the college of Sangpu, which first flourished under Ngok Loden Sherap, an excellent scholar of Sanskrit who was inspired by the rigor of Indian epistemological theories. The Sangpu curriculum was based on debate practice and the careful study of major doctrinal and philosophical works, particularly those of Dharmakīrti (ca. 600), whose logic served as the foundation for the system as a whole. Also emphasized were the Perfection of Wisdom or Prajñāpāramitā, the "meta-doctrine" or Abhidharma, the monastic code or Vinaya, and the Madhyamaka or "Middle Way" (Tib. *Uma*) teaching of the Indian master Nāgārjuna. Henceforth, these subjects, known as the "five great textual traditions" (*zhungchen-nga*), would become the core curriculum of the Tibetan monastic colleges, regardless of the order to which one belonged.

Although the study of these five topics required memorizing key Indian texts, instruction at Sangpu and its successors strongly emphasized learning through debate. Students mastered a Tibetan variation on Indian forms of argumentation that came to be known as *tel-chir*, "implication and reason," wherein an argument was expressed as an implication statement followed by the warranting reason, as in this example:

> *It is implied (tel)* that a vase is impermanent.
> *Because (chir)* it is composite.

Translated into Western schoolbook logic, this would read:
"a vase is a composite thing; all composite things are impermanent;
therefore, a vase is impermanent." This shows us, however, that
something seems missing from the Tibetan formulation, namely,
the explicit statement of the principle that "all composite things are
impermanent." This would be supplied if the debater's opponent
questioned the warranting reason, "because it is composite," in
which case the former might reply by adding:

> *It is implied* that composite things are impermanent.
> *Because,* as the Buddha has said, "all composite things are
> impermanent."

The Buddha's authority, invoked as a reason here, could also
be questioned, especially if the quotation was contradicted by
other scriptural citations. In actual debate practice, however,
adherence to purely logical criteria was seldom the rule: verbal
tricks might be employed to trap an opponent; and the debate
was always accompanied by vivid, ritualized gestures, partly
contrived to mimic a combat in which one might be hard put
to maintain his cool. (The point being, precisely, to learn to
remain calm under pressure.) In all events, the objective of a
debate was to win, and few, even among masters of the game,
might aspire to win consistently on the merits of the argument
alone. The training could be a painful and frustrating one,
as seen in the autobiography of a nineteenth-century teacher
from Amdo:

> On entering the monastic college, I studied the *Abbreviated Logic
> Course,* the way of reason. Because I didn't even understand the
> general application of the reason or implication, I was rejected by
> my companions and despairingly scolded by my teachers, who took
> to beating me harshly though it did no good at all.

6. Monks practicing debate in the courtyard of Ganden monastery, Tsongkhapa's seat in Central Tibet.

Debate encouraged able students to explore the implications of the texts they were simultaneously engaged in mastering. In some monastic colleges, the accent was placed less on debate and more on oral and written commentary, resembling the emphasis in some types of Western education on "explication de texte." Several pedagogical styles thus emerged, characterizing in part the approaches of differing monastic orders.

The emergence of Tibetan scholasticism

The Sangpu curriculum was refined by a succession of brilliant teachers, including Chapa Chökyi Senggé (1109–69), who is credited with systematizing the debate logic overall. Sakya Paṇḍita also received his early philosophical education at Sangpu before continuing his studies with the Kashmiri master Śākyaśrībhadra and his entourage of Indian scholars, with whom he applied

Four philosophical schools, five textual traditions

Following Indian sources, Tibetan Buddhists recognized four major philosophical schools, the first two representing the "Little Vehicle" (Hīnayāna) attributed to early Buddhism and the second two the "Great Vehicle" (Mahāyāna) that flourished beginning in the first centuries of the common era:

1. *Vaibhāṣika* (Tib. *jedrak mawa*) affirms an atomistic conception of reality and the theory that perception encounters its objects directly.
2. *Sautrāntika* (Tib. *dodépa*) believes that we perceive phenomenal forms caused by the interaction between objects and our sense organs, but that we do not directly perceive the objects that appear to us.
3. *Yogācāra* (Tib. *neljor chöpa, semtsam*) embraces a type of idealism, according to which subject and object are mere aspects of nondual cognition.
4. *Madhyamaka* (Tib. *uma*) argues that in the final analysis reality is beyond thought and speech, that even concepts such as "nondual cognition" mistakenly posit concrete absolutes where in fact no such thing can be affirmed. "Emptiness" serves to point to the intangible nature of reality but must itself not be grasped as an ultimate fact.

The perspectives of these four schools are studied in detail in the "five great textual traditions":

1. *Vinaya* (Tib. *dülwa*) primarily teaches the ethical discipline of the Vaibhāṣika.
2. *Abhidharma* (Tib. *ngönpa*) details the metaphysics of Vaibhāṣika, Sautrāntika and Yogācāra.
3. *Pramāṇa* (Tib. *tsema*)—logic and epistemology—is based on Sautrāntika and Yogācāra theory of knowledge.
4. *Prajñāpāramitā* (Tib. *parchin*)—the "Perfection of Wisdom"—investigates the Mahāyāna doctrines of the path

to enlightenment from the perspectives of both Yogācāra and Madhyamaka.

5. *Madhyamaka* (Tib. *uma*) introduces the insight into universal relativity and emptiness that characterizes the Madhyamaka philosophical system.

himself to mastering Sanskrit grammar and related subjects. This training would lend a notably "Indological" perspective to his mature scholarship. In his treatise, the *Scholar's Gate* (*Khepa Jukpé Go*), he sets forth his scholarly ideals in general, basing them on mastery of composition, rhetoric, and debate.

Indian traditions of logic and epistemology figured prominently among Sakya Paṇḍita's major concerns. His contributions included the revised Tibetan translation of Dharmakīrti's masterwork, the *Verse Commentary on Logic* (*Pramāṇavārttika*), and his own synthesis of Indian Buddhist epistemology, the *Treasury of Epistemic Reason* (*Tsema Rikter*). In other writings he commented at length on current doctrinal debates, voicing trenchant criticisms of various developments in Tibet. One of his foremost targets was the notion of sudden enlightenment, which he often characterized as the "Chinese Great Perfection." A rigorous adherence to canonical precepts was, for Sakya Paṇḍita, the touchstone of Buddhist practice:

> If you speak in accord with the Buddha's pronouncements you are a guru. If you practice in accord with his speech you are a disciple. If you achieve provisions that conform to them you are a patron. Where these are present, the teaching of the Buddha will be present as well.

The traditions of Sangpu and Sakya were largely responsible for the content, style, and method of subsequent Tibetan scholasticism, which came to be characterized by close study of the major Indian Buddhist philosophers—especially Nāgārjuna,

Asaṅga, and Dignāga, and their commentators Candrakīrti, Vasubandhu, and Dharmakīrti—rigorous adherence to methodical argument, and precise and elegant use of language. Nevertheless, skeptical undercurrents sometimes emerged. Thus, the second Karmapa hierarch, Karma Pakshi, authored a catalogue of disputed opinions in which he writes:

> It is held that saṃsāra has a beginning and end, and it is held that saṃsāra is without beginning or end. It is held that minds are of identical nature throughout all saṃsāra and nirvāṇa, and it is held that all minds are of differing natures. It is held that sentient beings are newly produced, and it is held that sentient beings are not newly produced. . . . But whatever such tenets—whether good, bad or mediocre—one might harbor are the causes of good, bad or mediocre [conditions of] saṃsāra. They are devoid of the life-force of nirvāṇa. Whatever tenets, hankerings, or particular philosophical positions you hold, they cause you to be buddhaless and make you meet with saṃsāra.

For thinkers like Karma Pakshi, it was an intuitive breakthrough achieved in contemplation, and not the elaboration of dogmatic systems, that revealed the true meaning of the Buddha's teaching.

At the same time, others attempted to reconcile these opposing trends—systematic and skeptical—in Buddhist thought. The fourteenth century saw a veritable eruption of interest in topics like "buddha-nature," "consciousness of the ground-of-all" (Skt. *ālayavijñāna*), and "luminous mind," all of which seemed to imply some fundamental reality besides "emptiness." This received its impetus in part from techniques of contemplation and yoga that made use of similar concepts, while the presence of these and related terms in some Indian writings led scholars to argue that the highest teachings of the Buddha were to be found only here. The debates this provoked were among the most contested areas of Tibetan Buddhist thought and among the richest in terms of the range of perspectives that emerged.

The third Karmapa Rangjung Dorjé contributed much here and set forth his views in a celebrated treatise, *Profound Inner Meaning (Zapmo Nangdön)*. The thinker most associated with controversial ontological speculations, however, was a junior contemporary of the Karmapa, Dölpopa Sherap Gyeltsen of the Jonangpa order, who asserted that emptiness was not the true nature of the absolute at all. This, he held, was in fact a plenitude and thus "extrinsically empty" (*zhentong*), that is, empty just of relative reality. Dölpopa's thinking—affirming that the Buddha taught the absolute to be permanent, eternal, self, and purity—sparked considerable controversy, and he was condemned by some as a tacit adherent of the Hindu teaching of the supreme self, *paramātman*. After the order to which he adhered, the Jonangpa, was suppressed during the 1650s by the fifth Dalai Lama, largely for political reasons, his writings were banned, and many believed the suppression to be due to perceived heresy. Nevertheless, Dölpopa's insistence that the absolute could not be conceived as a mere nothingness touched a sore nerve in Tibetan Buddhist thought, so that his teaching has been repeatedly revived, albeit with modifications, down to the present time.

The concepts of luminosity and buddha-nature are prominent, too, in the work of Longchen Rapjampa, the greatest exponent of the Nyingmapa teaching of the Great Perfection. Nowhere is this more evident than in his treatment of the "ground" (*zhi*), the basis for the actualization of the "fruit" (*drebu*) that is buddhahood. In his reflections on the emptiness of the absolute, he avoids Dölpopa's position but nevertheless also criticizes the apparently nihilistic tendencies of some Tibetan scholars. For Longchenpa, "emptiness" is the unconditioned, primordially pure character of ultimate reality, wherein buddhahood is an ever-present possibility. He thus resists Dölpopa's conclusion that emptiness is an extrinsic quality of a permanent absolute, while refusing to treat emptiness as a synonym for nothingness, with the nihilism that this would imply.

Three teachers on the absolute

Reality, or "suchness," is the ground of all saṃsāra and nirvāṇa, and is referred to by many names: the "primordial, indestructible, great seminal point," "Prajñāpāramitā," "inborn gnosis," and "ordinary cognition." When it is stirred by the agitating vital energy of intellect, extraneous thoughts grow active. Owing to the appearance of dichotomized phenomena, one adopts the convention [of distinguishing between] the "gnosis of the ground-of-all" (*ālayajñāna*) and the "consciousness of the ground-of-all" (*ālayavijñāna*)."

from Karmapa Rangjung Dorjé (1284–1339), *Profound Inner Meaning*

The intention is to distinguish intrinsic emptiness from extrinsic emptiness. Those who do not do so and . . . who maintain that all [the Buddha's] statements that ultimately there is existence, permanence, self, purity and truth are of provisional meaning, while all statements of nonexistence, impermanence, non-self, impurity and rottenness are of definitive meaning [merely indulge in] coarse and bad views, without number.

from Dölpopa (1292–1361), *Epistle to the Disciples*

Nowadays, most of the teachers and all of the hermits alike make out the ground to be a bare vacuity, nothing at all. . . . But by experientially cultivating a ground that is nothing at all, the fruit of awakening as a buddha, with all enlightened attributes, will not emerge, because the trio of ground, path and result has been confounded. . . . Here, it is the unconditioned and spontaneously present luminosity that is held to be the ground. If the inherent structure of such a ground is not recognized as it is, there comes to be unawareness. Due to that, having errantly constructed the apprehending subject and apprehended object, one wanders in the three realms.

from Longchen Rapjampa (1308–1363), *Distinguishing Consciousness from Gnosis*

7. The great fifteenth-century stūpa of Gyantsé, with its many interior chapels, arranged as a three-dimensional maṇḍala—the cosmos conceived as a divine palace—gives architectural expression to the cosmic vision of Tibetan Buddhism.

Tsongkhapa and his critics

The fourteenth century was a golden age for Tibetan Buddhist philosophy. Besides the figures just surveyed, a host of thinkers contributed to the elaboration of every aspect of Buddhist thought, engendering lively controversies in most areas. It became customary for aspirants to move from one center to another, studying with different masters and honing their debating skills on the way. One of those who entered this world of itinerant scholars as a youth was Jé Tsongkhapa Lozang Drakpa, later to be revered as the founder of the Gelukpa order. His dedication to the Kadampa teaching of the progressive path of the bodhisattva was such that he and his successors often came to be thought of as "new Kadampas," and his treatise the *Great Progression of the Path* is considered a definitive expression of this approach.

From his Sakyapa colleague, Rendawa Zhönnu Lodrö (1349–1412), he acquired special concern for the Prāsaṅgika, or "implicationist," interpretation of Nāgārjuna's Madhyamaka philosophy formulated by the Indian master Candrakīrti; for it is the hallmark of this approach to demonstrate universal relativity, or emptiness, only indirectly, by drawing out the implications of rival hypotheses. (Those who used direct proof to establish emptiness were by contrast known as Svātantrika, proponents of "autonomous argument.") It was in collaboration with Rendawa, moreover, that Tsongkhapa undertook a celebrated rehearsal of the monastic code, the Vinaya. He thoroughly rejected the "extrinsic emptiness" doctrine of Dölpopa, regarding it as exemplifying persistent Tibetan misunderstandings of the idealistic Yogācāra school of Indian Buddhist philosophy, and, though affirming the Prāsaṅgika interpretation of Madhyamaka, he developed his own unique understanding of it. In short, while drawing on earlier tradition, Tsongkhapa formulated a novel synthesis of the Indian Buddhist legacy, emphasizing careful textual study and the demands of logic.

Tsongkhapa clearly perceived that the many contested topics in the Buddhism of his day could not be resolved by appealing to scriptural authority alone and wrote:

> A scriptural passage which merely says "this [text] is of this [level of meaning]" cannot establish that to be so, for, as there is in general no invariable relationship [holding between such statements and the levels of meaning to which they refer], the mere statement, "this [scripture] is of this [level of meaning]" cannot prove a particular instance of interpretable or definitive meaning.

The would-be interpreter is therefore thrown back on reason if he is to cut through the conundrums posed by doctrinal texts. Contrary to those who believed that reason served only to refute wrong opinions but that it otherwise had no role on the Buddhist path, Tsongkhapa strongly affirmed the rational character of Buddhist teaching.

Tsongkhapa's commitment to reason pushed him to propose an innovative interpretation of Candrakīrti's philosophy, which provoked considerable dispute. To illustrate his approach, we mention briefly his arguments concerning the "consciousness of the ground-of-all," or *ālayavijñāna*. At issue is whether the Madhyamaka philosopher is required to affirm, even in relative terms, the existence of such a "ground" in order to explain the continuity of karma from one lifetime to the next. Tsongkhapa thought not and proposed to solve the problem of karma and causation by maintaining that the annihilation (*zhikpa*) of a thing could act in a causal stream just like a positive entity: it is a completed, that is to say, annihilated, deed that brings about the result. This may appear to be a rabbit pulled from the dialectical hat, and this, indeed, is just how his critics perceived it. Together with several other distinctive aspects of his thought, his thesis was universally rejected by those outside the Gelukpa order he had founded. One of his sharpest opponents, the Sakyapa Gorampa Sonam Senggé (1429–89), for instance, argued that it absurdly implied that "karma and its effects are totally different, since at the level of conventions, they are set off from one another by an intermediary, namely 'annihilation as a real entity,' just like two mountains that face each other are set off from one another by the river [that runs between them]." Much of the subsequent history of Buddhist thought in Tibet may be interpreted in terms of the continuing debate between Tsongkapa's critics and defenders.

Later developments

Political turmoil in Central Tibet during the seventeenth and eighteenth centuries, in tandem with Tibet's shifting relations with its Mongol and Manchu neighbors, contributed to important changes in Tibet's cultural geography, whereby new centers of intellectual and artistic activity emerged in Tibet's far eastern regions of Amdo and Kham.

Tsongkhapa on the study of logic

Some say that these treatises [of logic and epistemology] are merely useful in order to refute the misconceptions of the non-Buddhists, so that in places [like Tibet], where [non-Buddhists] are not present, there is no reason to study and to reflect upon them. But this undermines the teaching. . . . For these texts fully establish the means to refute such inflated opinions as those which hold there to be no former or past lives, no liberation or omniscience, and hold the aggregates to be pure, happy, permanent and self, etc. Therefore, even in this place where non-Buddhists are not present, you must consider introspectively whether or not you need to eliminate inflated opinions whereby you grasp your own aggregates as pure, happy, permanent and self, etc., and whether or not you need to achieve certainty in regard to past and future lives, liberation and omniscience, etc. And, if those be needed, you must indicate whether, [to achieve them,] there is any other means superior to these treatises on reason.

. . . and on causality and karma

Some hold that, if virtuous or unvirtuous deeds were to abide until the maturation of the result, then they would be permanent, so that [one who affirmed this] would fall into the extreme of eternalism, while if, on the other hand, the deed that was performed were to be annihilated in the second instant, then, because [something] annihilated cannot be an entity, it could not generate the mature result, wherefore completed deeds would vanish without trace.

Some respond to this argument, saying that, even though the deed be annihilated, there is a ground for the successive emergence of the potency of the deed, which is considered to be the ground-of-all, while others affirm this to be the continuous stream of intellectual consciousness. . . . Our own response is

that, even without affirming [such] propositions, it is implied that
the completed deed will not vanish without trace. For there is no
contradiction involved if we assume that it is the annihilated deed
that generates a result. . . . For though [something] annihilated
cannot be an entity if you affirm concrete particulars [to be the
defining type of entity], we do not affirm the concrete particular
even as a matter of convention, wherefore both annihilated and
unannihilated deeds are equivalent with respect to whether or not
they are entities.

The prominence of the East in this period is well illustrated in the
life and work of the notable eighteenth-century figure, Changkya
Rölpé Dorjé (1717–86). Born among the Monguor ethnic group
of Qinghai, he was identified at the age of four as the incarnation
of a famous lama and later sent by the Manchus to Beijing to be
educated at the court. There he became the fast friend of a Manchu
prince, who later succeeded to the throne as the emperor Qianlong
(r. 1736–99), the greatest of the Qing monarchs. Changkya rose
with his friend to become the empire's preeminent Buddhist
clergyman, as well as the confidant and biographer of the seventh
Dalai Lama Kelzang Gyatso (1708–57). As Changkya's writings
make clear, he adhered closely to Tsongkapa's ideal of reason in
seeking to resolve the conflicted points of Buddhist teaching. This
found its most sustained expression in Changkya's great synthesis
of Buddhist philosophies, *Philosophical Systems Beautifying the
World-Mountain*, which sought, so far as possible, to base itself
directly upon Indian sources. Nevertheless, Changkya's work was
in part motivated by his encounters with Chinese Buddhism and
his recognition that this tradition, differing in certain respects
from Tibetan Buddhism, emphasized aspects of the Indian
Buddhist legacy that had been relatively overlooked in Tibet.
His interest in philosophical systems was inherited by his
disciple and biographer, Tuken Chökyi Nyima (1737–1802), who
complemented his master's work with the *Crystal Mirror of*

Philosophical Systems, treating the peculiarly Tibetan systems of Buddhist thought and practice, and offering a detailed exposé of Chinese traditions, including Confucianism and Taoism as well.

In Kham, the nineteenth-century "nonpartisan" (*rimé*) movement sought to emphasize the complementarities, and not the divisions, among the various Tibetan orders and lineages. This outlook is well exemplified in the writings of Mipam Namgyel (1846–1912), who was convinced that Tibetan Buddhists had more in common than sectarian polemicists were willing to admit. In a satirical essay, after noting some of the strengths and vulnerabilities of the four major orders, he concluded that solidarity among them was the need of the day. Despite continuing sectarian rivalries, the tolerant outlook he expressed here has come to be broadly— though by no means universally—embraced in contemporary Tibetan Buddhist circles.

Mipam on nonsectarianism

In the teaching in general, though you may favour your own faction, it's most important not to hate the others. In thinking about your own faction, because you are followers of the Teacher, the Transcendent Lord Buddha alone, you must perceive one another as intimates. The philosophical systems of the teaching in Tibet began at the time of . . . the religious king [Tri Songdetsen]. From that ancient and excellent legacy, all [the Tibetan orders] are alike in affirming the four seals [the impermanence, suffering, and selflessness of conditioned things, and the peace of nirvāṇa] that mark the transmitted precepts of the teaching. Above and beyond that, all affirm great, unelaborate emptiness and, what's more, they also affirm the vehicle of the tantras [which teach] the coalescence of bliss and emptiness. Because, then, in point of fact, their views and systems are similar, they are exceedingly close.

In thinking about other factions, [consider that] next to non-Buddhists and barbarians, with whom we share not even tokens and dress, and who are [as numerous] as nighttime stars, we, who are just a few, are like daytime stars and are approaching the completion of the teaching. While something of it remains, those who have entered into the domains of the teaching with common purpose ought to cultivate the perception that they are most closely related. Because mutual enmity will bring ruination, regard one another as does a mother her child, or as does a begger a treasure, and so cultivate a perception of joy.

from Mipam Namgyel (1846–1912), *Surprises Due to a Conversation with Friends*

Chapter 6
Enlightenment in this very body

What is "Tantric Buddhism"?

Tibetan Buddhism is often characterized as "tantric," though seldom with careful definition. In several spheres, including monastic discipline and philosophical education, non-tantric teachings and practices were generally privileged. Despite this, Tibetan Buddhism was indebted to tantric traditions in aspects of popular and monastic ritual, and yoga and meditation were most often tantric as well. But just how is "tantra" understood in Tibet? The question is not an easy one to answer and was much debated among Tibetan authorities themselves.

Though precise definition is elusive, some characteristics of Buddhist tantra are widespread. Peltrül Rinpoché (d. 1887), a famous Nyingmapa author, raises the issue while discussing how the disciple should attend to his teacher's lessons. According to the exoteric sūtras, he says, the student cultivates motivation, respectful comportment, careful memorization, and similar qualities. None of this is rejected by the tantras, but they add this difference: instead of regarding your teacher, yourself, and your classmates as ordinary human beings, you learn to perceive the learning environment as an awakened realm, in which the teacher *is* the Buddha or presiding divinity, and you and your classmates *are* the enlightened disciples, or the gods and goddesses, of the retinue. The teaching itself, transcending the mundane here and now, is the perpetual flow of the Buddha's insight, continuously received by those receptive to it. In other words, in the way of the sūtras, one is to cultivate positive qualities as causes for future enlightenment, but in the tantras, the fruit of enlightenment is already here. The tantras teach us to perceive the ordinary world as a buddha-realm. Hence, Tibetan authorities often speak of the sūtras as teaching a *causal vehicle*, while the tantras present the *vehicle of fruition*.

Although this helps to introduce the general ethos of tantra, it remains still vague. Is the idea that buddhahood is ever-present sufficient to count as tantra? Few in the Tibetan traditions would agree. It is in seeking greater precision that the characterization of tantra becomes controversial. Without proposing a strict definition, a number of frequently invoked features merit consideration.

Mantra: The use of spell-like formulae, called *dhāraṇī*, or *mantra* (Tib. *ngak*) is pervasive in the tantras, so that their teaching is often called *mantrayāna*, the "mantra vehicle." While many non-tantric Buddhist sūtras employ *dhāraṇī*, particularly as mnemonic formulae, in tantric contexts mantras pervade all aspects of ritual and contemplation. Thus, the twelfth-century Sakyapa teacher, Sachen Künga Nyingpo, defines the word "mantra" as meaning "that which protects the mind," and further explains: "By being skilled in the stages of creation and perfection, sensory consciousness, and what flows from it, is protected from intellectual engagement in mundane discursive thought." (The terms "creation" and "perfection" refer here to the two major phases of tantric practice, the first emphasizing creative visualization and ritual, and the second involving the perfection of the adept's identification with the visualized deity through exercises of internal yoga.)

Maṇḍala: Though the term *maṇḍala* (Tib. *kyinkhor*) is current outside of tantric contexts to refer to ordered arrangements, including the well-appointed array of a buddha and his divine and human disciples, in the tantras it designates specifically a type of diagram—usually either painted on cloth or made of colored powders sprinkled on a flat surface, and more rarely modeled three-dimensionally—that schematically represents the divine palace of a particular buddha, bodhisattva, or deity, accompanied by his or her divine circle of attendants. This is symbolically correlated, moreover, with the macrocosmic universe and with the microcosm of the individual. Thus, for instance, a maṇḍala of five deities may be taken to correspond to the five bundles, or *skandhas*, the basic elements of which a living being is formed, or to the five elements—earth, water, fire, air, and space—composing the material world as a whole.

Abhiṣeka: Entry into the tantras requires a particular consecration ritual, called *abhiṣeka* (Tib. *wangkur*), "aspersion," whereby the disciple is initiated by the guru into the maṇḍala of a particular buddha, bodhisattva, or deity. As Sachen Künga Nyingpo tells us, "one may practice after body, speech, and mind are consecrated as the indestructible reality (*vajra*) of buddha-body, -speech, and -mind." Without obtaining *abhiṣeka* and assenting to the special vows (Skt. *samaya*, Tib. *damtsik*) that this entails, one is not authorized to undertake the ritual or contemplative practices of the tantras.

Visualization, the creative use of the imagination, is employed in all branches of Buddhism, affording powerful means to further meditation. Tantric visualizations are related to the principle of the maṇḍala, often involving the meditator's imagined identification with its central divinity. As Sachen explains, "Concerning skill in the means of one's favored deity, one transforms oneself into that deity. All objects, form and so forth, that appear, are likewise made into the deity. Then, one's enjoyment [of objects] is like deity melting into deity. The beginner just practices self-identification [with the deity], and, attaining stability of mind, learns to make the features clear." Corresponding to the requirement of clear visualization, one may note a degree of iconographic elaboration, involving divinities who may be male or female, benign or demonic, of any color, and often endowed with many legs, heads, and arms, wielding the weapons, ritual objects, and sacred substances with which they are associated, ritually and symbolically.

Ritual: Buddhist tantra is distinguished from other forms of Buddhism by the extreme elaboration of its rituals, which developed in India under the influence of the ancient traditions of the Vedas and of Hindu tantrism. Characteristic of tantric rituals are complex altar arrangements, involving manifold offerings, representations, and symbolic objects; intricate programs of liturgical chant, punctuated by use of mantras and special gestures (Skt. *mudrā*); and stipulations regarding concentration (Skt. *samādhi*) to engender a visualized ritual program corresponding to outer ritual performance. Specifications pertain to the practitioner's clothing and ornaments, and the details of instruments and implements including drums, horns, and the ubiquitous vajra and bell. (The *vajra* [Tib. *dorjé*], a type of scepter identified as both diamond and lightning bolt, is the most widespread symbol of esoteric Buddhism and represents the indestructibility and brilliance of the enlightened mind.)

Sensual pleasures are to be affirmed, not renounced. Sachen, like many authorities, proposes that this is a fundamental distinction between the exoteric Mahāyāna sūtras and the esoteric tantras: "The proclamation of two paths is intended for two types of individual. Some are unconcerned with sensual pleasures and so are able to abandon them. For them, the vehicle of the transcendent perfections [taught in the sūtras] was proclaimed. Others are greatly preoccupied by sensory pleasures and so unable to abandon them, and for them the vehicle of indestructible reality was proclaimed." However, the affirmation of the senses in tantric rituals is not an authorization of ordinary sensual indulgence. Tantric engagement in sensual phenomena is subservient not to whims and desires but to precise ritual programs. Sachen's explanation thus continues: "Those who have entered the vehicle of secret mantra, being skilled in both the stage of creation and that of perfection, may rely upon sensual pleasures. For example, according to the tantras, the eye is made into [the bodhisattva] Kṣitigarbha, and all form is made into [the goddess] Rūpavajrā. One thereby enjoys [vision] in the manner of deity embracing deity, and similarly sound and smell, etc., are all enjoyed as is appropriate."

Yoga: In the highest practices of tantra, outer ritual receives less emphasis than the esoteric techniques of yoga (Tib. *neljor*). "Yoga" in this case is not the gymnastic yoga widely taught these days in health clubs. It refers, rather, to practices of meditation through which the adept may achieve union (Skt. *yoga*) with the highest reality. Tantric practices of creative visualization are thus thought of as "deity yoga" and the recitation of the deity's mantra as "recitation yoga." In the so-called perfection stage of tantric practice, the focus turns to the subtle energies of the body, conceived as a network of energy channels concentrated at vital points called "wheels" (Skt. *cakra*, Tib. *khorlo*). Whereas, among ordinary persons, these subtle energies are dispersed and uncoordinated, by means of tantric yoga they are united in the central channel, bringing about swift liberation. Because modern gymnastic yoga is ultimately derived from medieval Indian tantric systems, similar concepts remain familiar in the general milieu of contemporary yoga practice. However, in Buddhist tantra, the internal yogas are primarily contemplative techniques, corresponding to particular tantras with their specific maṇḍalas and deities.

Transgression is sometimes also regarded as characteristic of tantric practice. Adepts may indulge in what, in other contexts, is considered unclean or polluting, for instance, consuming excrement or forbidden meats, taking intoxicants, or seeking spiritual bliss through sexual enjoyment. Not all Buddhist tantras encourage such actions, and many Tibetan authorities shunned these aspects of the tantras altogether. Although Indian understandings of tantric transgression have been disputed in recent scholarship, in Tibet there was broad consensus that the transgressions mentioned in the texts were usually to be treated symbolically, as their actual practice pertained only to small numbers of highly advanced adepts. Even among the latter, the transgressions were to be carefully constrained and limited to precise ritual contexts. Thus, for instance, at the tantric feasts—literally the "wheel of the assembly" (Skt. *gaṇacakra*, Tib. *tsokkhor*)—of the tenth and twenty-fifth days of the month, small morsels of meat and a few drops of alcohol may be served to participants as tokens of the transgressions whereby the great adepts of the past, such as Padmasambhava, transcended all dualistic bounds to attain supreme realization. Nevertheless, the ritual of the feast remains rigidly codified, so that even its "transgressions" conform to a perfectly orchestrated routine. Hence, tantric transgression, as understood in Tibet, is not at all antinomian, but is part of an ordered system.

Secrecy: The conception of the tantras as "esoteric" is directly related to the frequent ascription to them of secrecy. This may be taken literally to mean that their teachings and practices are to be concealed from the uninitiated, but often also allusively, indicating that only those who are suitably receptive can gain insight into the tantras, whether or not they are deliberately concealed.

Not all of these nine features are present whenever Tibetan Buddhists speak of tantra, though the first four generally are. Tantra is best thought of not as a fixed phenomenon but as a broad and complex category, whose constituents are linked by a range of properties that are variously shared and divided among them.

Stages of tantric practice

Leaving definition aside, tantra in Tibet is more a matter of practice than of theory and in practice is invariably transmitted directly from master to disciple. As the great yogi and poet

Four classes of tantras

In contrast to the Bönpo and Nyingmapa, who classify their tantric teachings variously within their systems of "nine vehicles," most of the other traditions of Tibetan Buddhism have adopted a system with four classes of tantras (*gyüdé zhi*):

1. Kriyātantra (Tib. *jawé gyü*, "tantras of ritual action") and (2) Caryātantra (Tib. *chöpé gyü*, "tantras of conduct") emphasize rituals for purification and protection, in which the adept enters into a temporary relationship with the divinity for the duration of the ritual performed. They differ in general in the degree of the elaboration of their consecrations and other rites.
3. Yogatantra (Tib. *neljor-gi gyü*, "tantras of yoga") further develops the practitioner's contemplative identification with the divinity, while in (4) Anuttara- (or Niruttara-) yogatantra (Tib. *neljor lamé gyü*, "unexcelled Yogatantra") a permanent identification is sought, and the accent shifts from ritual to internal disciplines of yoga.

The relationship between adept and deity in these four classes of practice is sometimes compared to that between lovers: first exchanging glances and smiles; then holding hands and playing innocent games; next hugs and kisses; finally the intimacy and bliss of union.

Milarepa is always considered the exemplary disciple, his story will help us to understand tantra as part of Tibetan religious experience.

After practicing sorcery during his youth in order to avenge the hardships inflicted on his family by a cruel uncle, Mila began to regret the sufferings he caused through his success in the black arts. Motivated to achieve liberation, he sought Buddhist teachings from several masters, but little good came of it. Upon hearing the name of the translator Marpa, however, he was moved by great faith and so journeyed to meet him. Marpa, for his part, recognized Milarepa's potential as soon as he saw him but was careful not to let this be known. As a Tibetan proverb states, "the disciple's faith is the ring that catches the hook of the teacher's compassion." Tantric practice must be grounded in unswerving devotion to a qualified teacher; without this, only its outer forms survive.

But faith alone is not sufficient to ready the disciple for initiation. Marpa was aware of Milarepa's potential but saw too that, owing to past sins, he was not yet a fit vessel for the teaching. He therefore demanded that Milarepa undergo harsh trials, virtually serving as Marpa's slave, until, when all trace of pride was broken, he was at last purified and suitably prepared. Initiated into the maṇḍala of the deity Cakrasaṃvara, he was instructed in the corresponding esoteric yogas, derived from the "Six Teachings of Nāropa," above all the exercise of the subtle energies known as the "wild woman" (*tummo*), the inner heat, mastery of which allowed him to remain in the wilderness throughout the harsh Tibetan winter with only a light cotton robe. ("Repa," which became part of his name and was subsequently adopted by many of his disciples as well, literally means "cotton-clad.") Through years of privation in solitary retreat he strove to master this discipline, together with the remaining "Six Teachings," through which he came to realize the apparitional nature of existence and the visionary possibilities of lucid dreaming in relation to the radiance of the mind. In the end, he was believed to have become a buddha; he had succeeded in attaining the tantras' goal of enlightenment in "a single lifetime, a single body."

Adepts such as Milarepa are rare, and so too teachers such as Marpa, who perceive the specific needs of their disciples and instruct them accordingly. More often training in the tantras is practiced following well-established patterns, although the disciple's faith in a formally qualified master is always an essential prerequisite.

Instead of the trials that Milarepa endured, most disciples undertake the more predictable challenge of the preliminary practices (*ngöndro*). All tantric rituals involve preliminaries such as arranging the altar and the offerings, consecrating the ritual implements, and the first steps of the ritual itself, including the Buddhist refuge and the cultivation of *bodhicitta*, the compassionate spirit of enlightenment. In the present context, however, the preliminaries are obligatory spiritual exercises that may take anywhere from a few months to a year to complete. Typically, they commence with the contemplation of fundamental Buddhist themes: the unique opportunity of human existence; death and impermanence; the sufferings of beings in saṃsāra; and the operations of karma. A period of reflection, often in retreat, devoted to these is followed by a series of practices including the performance of one hundred thousand repetitions of the refuge, accompanied, with each repetition, by a full prostration, one hundred thousand repetitions of the vow of the bodhisattva, and, similarly, one hundred thousand repetitions each of the hundred-syllable purificatory mantra of the Buddha Vajrasattva, of the offering of the maṇḍala (here meaning a symbolic representation of the cosmos), and of the formula of *guruyoga*, the worship of the divinized guru. The qualities cultivated by these practices—renunciation, compassion, purity, and faith—qualify the student as a suitable candidate for the major tantric practices. Following his or her initiation into the maṇḍala of the deity—and the choice of deity depends above all on the specific lineage into which one is initiated—these begin with the creation stage, in which the visualization of the deity and recitation of its mantra are cultivated. This is usually to be practiced for a prolonged period in retreat, requiring the performance of a fixed number of repetitions of the mantra, together with a variety of rituals cementing one's relation with the deity. Mastery of the creation stage is the prerequisite for the perfection practices, as exemplified by the "Six Teachings of Nāropa."

At the culmination of the tantric path, elaborate ritual and the intricate disciplines of internal yoga give way to simplicity, as the adept focuses upon the examination of the reality underlying all possible experiences. The subtle radiance of mind finds its ground in emptiness and is identified with the *dharmakāya*, the all-embracing "body of reality" of the buddhas. In the Kagyüpa and allied traditions, the contemplation of the ultimate at this stage of practice is the Mahāmudrā, the "Great Seal," while among the Nyingmapa and Bönpo it is the Dzokchen, or "Great Perfection." Though these approaches each have numerous particular features, according to the distinct tantric systems to which they appertain, they share a common outlook reflecting the preeminence of Madhyamaka thought in Mahāyāna Buddhist milieux. As summarized in a prayer by the third Karmapa Rangjung Dorjé:

> Free from intellectual contrivance,
>> this is the Mahāmudrā;
> Without limiting parameters,
>> it is the great Madhyamaka;
> As the gathering point of all,
>> it's also called "Great Perfection"—
> With confidence may we realize
>> the one knowledge embracing all!

Institutional and social entailments

Just as tantra is regularly taught through a progressed path involving well-defined stages of practice, so the circumstances for tantric teaching have come to be largely institutionalized. Most Tibetan Buddhist orders maintain a system of "tantric colleges" complementing the dialectical colleges in which philosophical subjects are taught. Among the Nyingmapa and Kagyüpa orders, for instance, training in the tantras is typically conducted in a center of retreat (*drupdra*), wherein the trainees are sequestered for a period of three years and three fortnights (*losum choksum*), during which they practice in turn, under the guidance of the retreat master, the preliminaries and the stages of creation and perfection, culminating with the teachings of the Mahāmudrā or Dzokchen. Among the Gelukpa, however, the tantric college (*gyüdé dratsang*) has a more academic profile, combining training in ritual practice with progressive study of the tantric scriptures upon which Gelukpa ritual traditions are based. In either case, the collective retreat or tantric college is not seen as the end of training in the tantras but as a beginning: the most highly motivated disciples may go on to spend long years in solitary retreat, emulating past adepts such as Milarepa.

An important institution, too, is the Ngakpa Dratsang, the "College of Mantra-adepts (*ngakpa*)." The "mantra-adepts" here are ordained lay priests, often within the Nyingmapa order, who attend to a broad range of rituals required for the peace and prosperity of the surrounding community. In many cases, Ngakpa Tratsangs enjoy a relation of complementarity with a neighboring Gelukpa temple or monastery. This symbiosis of celibate monasticism and lay tantrism is a legacy of the fifth Dalai Lama, whose twin allegiances to the Gelukpa and Nyingmapa traditions resulted in his nurturing the latter, even as he promoted the former in tandem with the development of the Tibetan state.

In tantric Buddhism, the most crucial relationship is that between guru, or lama, and disciple. The disciple pledges body, speech, and mind to the teacher who bestows consecration upon him, and one's oath to the teacher is inviolable. By entering into a teacher's circle, you become similarly bound by oath to your fellow disciples, who thus become "vajra brothers and sisters." Although such relations could not be uniformly maintained, Tibetans traditionally took them very seriously, and few charges against a person were more damaging of reputation than that of being one who had violated *samaya*, the tantric vows.

The importance of oath-bound relations in tantric Buddhism had important social implications. One feature that Tibet shared with many feudal societies was the important role of sworn oaths and

8. A lay priest (*ngakpa*) at a Nyingmapa tantric college in Amdo. The structure to his *left* is the *sangtap* in the college's courtyard, the special furnace used for *sang*, the fumigation of the environment through the offering of aromatic substances.

the obligations that were derived from them. This was an essential characteristic of Tibetan culture quite apart from Buddhism and is much emphasized, for instance, in Tibetan epic literature. With the development of tantric Buddhism in Tibet, there emerged a degree of congruence between lamas and lords. Of course, not all who were respected as religious teachers held worldly rank, nor were more than a small proportion of the nobles ever regarded as spiritual masters as well. But in a significant number of cases lord and lama were one—the hierarchy of the Sakyapa order provides a clear instance. Under such circumstances, the tantric vow, binding master and disciples into a single spiritual family, served in effect to supercharge the relation of fealty, which was now reinforced not merely by the social approval or disapproval attached to it but by the menace of swift rebirth in the infernal realms to any who transgressed their commitments.

9. Dancers at a performance of *cham*, ritual masked dance, at the Tramdruk temple in Central Tibet. Although *cham* may have its origins in indigenous Tibetan cults of the local protective deities, its practice has been entirely reformulated over the centuries to conform with the ritual strictures of the tantras.

With the development of identified incarnation (*trülku*) as the means to ensure monastic succession, a process culminating in the transformation of Tibet itself into an ecclesiastical state headed by one such incarnation line, that of the Dalai Lamas, the tantric vow became a fundamental instrument binding Tibetan society as a whole. The great network of Gelukpa monasteries, and often establishments of other orders as well, was led by churchmen who were themselves bound to the Dalai Lamas by their vows. The system of recognized incarnation meant that the connections and obligations thereby created were maintained over the course of generations. In this way, the formerly exceptional relationship of tantric master and disciple became an instrument of social cohesion.

As tantrism suffused the social order, so too the very fabric of space and time. Thus the pilgrimage landscape of Tibet came to be conceived in terms of the principle of the maṇḍala—Mount Kailash, for instance, was regarded as the palace of the great tantric deity Cakrasaṃvara, in the center of a maṇḍala inscribed in the lakes, rivers, mountains, and caves for hundreds of miles around. Indeed, those of "pure vision" might journey to hidden lands (*beyül*), where terrestrial paradises were to be found. And the rituals marking the festival cycles were also tantric in most cases; often these were accompanied by masked dances, *cham*, in which the deities of the maṇḍala were manifest to the eyes of all.

Chapter 7
When this life ends

Among the Tamang people of Nepal, it is sometimes said that for weddings one must send for a brahman priest, but that a funeral must be officiated by a lama. Tibetan Buddhism is regarded as having a special command of mortuary ritual and the means to assure a fortunate rebirth for the deceased. The prominence of mortuary cult in Tibet reflects the confluence of both indigenous and Buddhist beliefs and practices, as these have intermingled and developed for more than a thousand years.

The uncertain fate of the dead

Archaeology and early Tibetan writings demonstrate the importance to pre-Buddhist Tibet of mortuary rites. The *Old Tibetan Chronicle*, composed ca. 800, opens with an account of the death of the first mortal king, Drigum Tsenpo, and describes the origins of royal interment: the monarch's hair was to be braided and his face painted with vermillion; his body was preserved in a mausoleum, with offerings of food and drink. Other documents discovered at Dunhuang also detail the program at royal funerals, which required an elaborate and specialized priesthood, and often followed the death by several years. These were solemn moments for the old Tibetan monarchy, and later Tibetan historiography reflects this in its scrupulous attention to the construction and placement of the mausoleums of early kings, which have remained hallowed places of pilgrimage.

The careful attendance of the dead, their provision with adequate nutrition, and traditions concerning the bodily ascent of the kings prior to Drigum Tsenpo to the heavens—these demonstrate that there were clear Tibetan beliefs concerning the fate of the dead prior to the advent of Buddhism. Just what those beliefs were, however, remains uncertain. It is possible that reincarnation, at least in the event of neonatal death, was affirmed, suggesting the concept of a persisting soul. Nevertheless, several of the earliest Tibetan Buddhist documents clearly treat the Buddhist idea of a repeating cycle of birth, death, and rebirth as alien to earlier belief. One example is *The Cycle of Birth and Death*, a poem that begins with the discovery of death by the Tibetan gods, one of whom, Precious Jewel, becomes profoundly upset on learning that his father, Light Blazing King, is dying; he searches throughout the universe for the means to overcome this terrible situation. He ultimately finds the goal of his quest in India, meeting with the Buddha, Śākyamuni, who assuages the gods' fears by teaching them a tantric funeral ritual, which will insure future well-being for the deceased.

From the late-tenth century on, Tibet absorbed newly transmitted rituals and contemplative practices from India, including many that were intended to forestall death or to guarantee that the deceased would realize an auspicious path. Accordingly, funerary rites of Tibetan authorship responded to these new inputs. The so-called *Tibetan Book of the Dead*, revealed as "spiritual treasure" (*terma*) in the fourteenth century, is surely the most famous product of this process.

Of central importance here was the conception of the *bardo* (Skt. *antarābhava*), the "intermediate state" between death and rebirth. The idea originated in Indian Buddhism in response to problems raised concerning the Buddhist denial of an enduring

The Ars Moriendi in Tibet

A fourteenth-century "treasure" attributed to Padmasambhava offers these counsels to prepare for death:

> After the earth element [in the body] dissolves into water, the body grows heavy, and cannot be supported. When water dissolves into fire, the mouth and nose dry out. When the fire dissolves into wind, bodily heat is lost. When wind dissolves into consciousness, breath is forced out in a sudden exhalation, and you can't accept the offerings you're given to swallow. At that time, you feel that you're being pressed down by a great mountain, or that you've been forced into darkness, or thrown into empty space, and all appearance is accompanied by whirring and hissing noises. The entire atmosphere becomes glaringly bright, as if a silken canopy were thrown open. In a tent of rainbow-light one's awareness seems to fill up space with peaceful and wrathful and semi-wrathful [spirits], who have various sorts of heads and forms, and wield all sorts of weapons, roaring in all sorts of ferocious tones. . . . And the light that shines is like a hundred-thousand suns rising at once.

> At that time, know this: the thought that you are being crushed is not a mountain oppressing you, for it is the dissolution of your own physical elements. Don't be frightened by that! The thought that you are being forced into darkness is not darkness, for it is the dissolution of your own five sensory organs. The thought that you are falling through space is not falling, for when mind and body part, and breath ceases, mind is without support. All manifestations of rainbow-light are the radiance of your own awareness. All peaceful and wrathful embodiments are forms of your own awareness. All sounds are its natural sound. All the lights are its natural light. Have no doubt about it! For if you doubt, you'll be thrown into saṃsāra.

Introducing the Moment of Death, a treasure of Dorjé Lingpa self or soul, in the absence of which the connection between one life and the next seemed inexplicable. The concept of a passage linking successive lives was embraced by some schools as a plausible solution, and it was this theory that was adopted as the *bardo* in Tibet.

The notion of the *bardo* was not just theoretical, however. In some tantras, a process was described in which the deceased experienced various sounds and lights, to which he or she reacted with fear or attraction, thereby setting the course to a new birth. Special meditations were developed to prepare for these experiences, so that one might be assured a safe journey culminating in fortunate rebirth.

With the promotion of such instructions in Tibet, funerary rites based on them were elaborated, incorporating what may have been an indigenous Tibetan funerary custom of calling the dead. The meditations of the *bardo* were no longer the exclusive domain of the adept, but could be imparted by a priest reading a guide to the *bardo* during the period when the deceased's consciousness was thought to be still wandering within it. With the great distribution of the *Book of the Dead*—in Tibetan the "Great Liberation by Hearing in the Bardo" (*Bardo tödröl*)—and similar works, such beliefs came to pervade Tibetan conceptions of the fate of the dead.

The pure lands

If you were able to choose your course of rebirth, what would you choose? Certainly, birth in the hells or among tormented ghosts must be avoided; so too animal existences, subject as they are, according to Buddhist views, to short lifespan, terror, pain, and stupidity. The gods and titans enjoy great power, longevity, and heavenly pleasures, but they are subject, in the end, to the decline of their merits and an inescapable fall into inferior realms. And human life is considered to be really favorable only if one has the capacity and inclination to enter the Buddha's path, together with the resources to do so. For consciousness wandering in the *bardo*, terrified by sounds and lights, the prospects therefore appear dismal.

By all means, then, one should either put an end to rebirth by attaining nirvāṇa, or else seek rebirth in a realm where one can learn and practice the Dharma and thus progress to eventual liberation. Many such options seem available. In the Tuṣita heaven, Maitreya, the coming Buddha, is already crowned as regent and teaches the Dharma to the gods. In the mysterious land of Shambhala, somewhere to the north, the kings preserve the *Tantra of the Wheel of Time* and prepare for world conquest. On Mount Potalaka, Avalokiteśvara, the bodhisattva of compassion, holds court; while on the isle of ogres the great adept Padmasambhava will teach the tantras until the end of the eon.

One should never make travel plans in haste, however. To be born in the presence of Maitreya, one requires the merits of a god. Only advanced adepts will reach Shambhala, and to join Padmasambhava one risks birth among the ogres instead of among human disciples. On close examination, even most Buddhist paradises are therefore not without risk. It is for this reason that one destination is favored over all: Sukhāvatī (Tib. *Dewachen*), the Land of Bliss to the west presided over by the Buddha of endless light, Amitābha (Tib. *Öpamé*). For this Buddha's vow stipulates that all those who have faith in him and his realm, and who have been morally upright, will be born in his presence on this basis alone, without need for the merits of a god or the attainments of an advanced meditator.

The teachings of the buddha Amitābha and his Sukhāvatī realm began in early first millennium India but soon spread to China and enjoyed enormous success throughout East Asia, giving rise to "Pure Land Buddhism," which is sometimes portrayed as resonating with Christian spirituality owing to its emphasis on the devotee's faith and the Buddha's grace. In Tibet, however, there was no sectarian development of this sort; instead, all of the Tibetan Buddhist orders affirmed rebirth in the Land of Bliss as a preeminent, though not exclusive, spiritual goal. Innumerable tantric as well as exoteric devotions, meditations, and rituals were composed to ensure this happy outcome.

On preparing for rebirth as one sleeps

At night, when going to sleep, lie down upon your right side. Perform the refuge and cultivation of *bodhicitta*, and thinking to yourself that this very place is the Sukhāvatī realm, visualize yourself as your favored meditational deity. Visualize that before you, atop a lotus and lunar disk, sits Amitābha, red in color, his hands resting in an even gesture and holding a begging bowl filled with ambrosia. He sits in the cross-legged posture, adorned with jewel-ornaments. Think that he is surrounded by the gurus. Then, thinking that all around them are the buddhas and bodhisattvas, mentally perform three prostrations. . . . Then, together with your exhalations, imagine that your mind dissolves into the heart of the Conqueror, indivisibly merging with the Conqueror's heart. When you inhale, imagine that light comes forth from the Conqueror's heart, and entering by the path of your speech, dissolves into your heart, so that the Conqueror's Mind and your mind indivisibly merge. After practicing that for three cycles [of breath], imagine that the buddhas and bodhisattvas dissolve into the gurus and the gurus then into Amitābha. Amitābha melts into light and dissolves into yourself. And you, in turn, dissolve into light, thinking the trinity of Buddha, meditational deity, and your own mind to be indivisibly intermingled. . . . Go to sleep in that state, without letting your thoughts wander. . . . By practicing this, in the future, sloughing off this body like a serpent's skin, you will be miraculously born from a lotus in Sukhāvatī in the west, and hear the Dharma preached by Amitābha.

Sleep Meditation on Amitābha, by Sakya Paṇḍita (1182–1251)

The most powerful means to direct one's course at death was generally considered to be the practice of *powa*, "transference," a tantric exercise intended to cause the consciousness of the dying individual to depart suddenly from the body through a forced opening at the crown of the skull, whence it may travel immediately to a desired realm. Although, once again, this was initially a technique reserved for virtuoso practitioners, at some point it came to be popularized and, like the teachings of the *bardo*, could be performed on one's behalf by a suitably qualified priest. Because adepts of *powa* were believed to be able to direct the consciousness to a blessed realm, the technique became not only an essential aspect of personal religious practice but equally the stock in trade for ritual specialists called upon to assist at the time of death and for the subsequent funeral rites. Thus its performance became a major source of religious revenue. Inevitably, given the devotional focus upon Amitābha's Land of Bliss, this came to be the preferred destination for the *powa* ritual as well.

Funeral customs

In Tibetan society the manner of one's death is a matter of great importance. Ideally, one should be comfortable and calm, and, if too ill to undertake appropriate religious practices oneself, at least able to understand when friends, family members, or, preferably, a lay priest or monk whisper instructions in one's ear to visualize one's teachers and to mentally perform devotions to the deities upon whom one has previously meditated. Those in attendance seek to ensure that the dying be in a tranquil and virtuous state of mind, for final thoughts contribute greatly to one's future destination. Immediately following death, the corpse is not to be touched until the *powa* has been performed. Lamps are to be kept constantly alight surrounding the deceased, and family members adopt the formal signs of mourning, leaving their hair disheveled, abandoning ornaments, and wearing old clothes.

If at all possible, a lama known to be a master of *powa* is invited to perform the rite in the presence of the deceased, but if this is not practical, the rite may be performed from afar. After some hours have passed, it is permitted to handle the corpse, and those who are charged to do so first touch the crown of the head, a sign of the departure of consciousness effected by the *powa*. As these and subsequent funerary activities are conducted, it is customary, too, to invite monks to the household to perform constant prayers on behalf of the departed. All clergy who participate in the last rites are to receive generous donations, for it is essential to demonstrate and augment the merits of the deceased in this way. An astrologer may also be consulted to prepare a death horoscope, and to determine what special rites need to be undertaken.

Once the corpse can be handled, it is bathed with fragrant water and wrapped in clean cloth, its orifices blocked with butter. It must also be bound with cords made of plant fiber, a means to render it immobile and thus incapable of being possessed by a zombie. As this clearly suggests, Tibetan mortuary practices, like last rites in other cultures, are as much concerned to assuage the anxieties of the living as they are to secure the peace of the dead. On the eve of the date determined by the astrologer for the disposal of the corpse, special efforts are made to multiply merits by making sure that prayers are recited and plentiful lamps and incense offered at neighboring shrines, following which the corpse will be removed from its former home, never to return.

The deceased departs on his or her final journey before dawn. Though interment and burial in rivers were known, the favored means of disposal in Tibet were cremation and "oblation for the birds (*jator*)," usually called "sky burial" in English, a euphemism for the dismemberment of the corpse at a designated charnel ground, where the remains are fed to vultures. It is not clear when this custom, which has a marked affinity with burial by exposure as practiced in the Zoroastrian religion, first became widespread in Tibet, but it has certainly been the preferred means in recent centuries. Cremation, however, is frequently practiced in lower elevation, forested regions, and in particular in areas such as Ladakh, Bhutan, and Nepal, which are closely contiguous with the sphere of Hindu civilization. Cremation is also often employed to dispose of the remains of lamas and other dignitaries.

The practice of sky burial was first noted by European travelers in the Middle Ages, and they interpreted it as evidence of cannibalism, imagining that bone implements used in some tantric rituals were the gruesome remains of departed parents. In fact, Tibetans regard the sky burial as an event of great solemnity, the last and ultimate offering one can make, a sacrifice of one's own flesh to feed hungry creatures who bear the matter of which one was made to pure celestial realms. Similarly, when cremation is practiced it is treated as a form of *homa*, the ancient Indian ritual of offering sacrifices into the flames, thereby transporting to heaven what is burned. The disposal of the corpse is both a final, culminating act of generosity and a passage to higher stations.

Following the custom said to have been introduced by the Chinese princess Jincheng during the eighth century, weekly observances are held for a period of seven weeks, culminating in elaborate ceremonies marking the forty-ninth day after death, at which point the deceased is supposed to have completed his or her passage through the *bardo* and to have reached the point of rebirth. After this, a service to mark the first anniversary of death is often performed and, in some cases, a regular annual memorial.

Throughout this entire period, Tibetan families place considerable emphasis on demonstrating their unstinting commitment to merit-making activities on behalf of the departed. At present, parental funerals are as enthusiastically documented in photography and video as are weddings in the United States, the reason for this being that "people should know that we have done well by our parents." As this makes clear, rebirth is thought to be determined, not as normative Buddhist doctrine would have us believe by the weight of one's personal karma alone, but also according to the merit that is generated on one's behalf, particularly by one's descendants.

Saintly death

Death, for Tibetans, is an incisive index of how one has lived. A serene passing contrasts sharply with dying in agony, a sense of closure following a life well lived with feelings of dismay and regret. The events leading up to and surrounding death, including the entire ensemble of mortuary rites, constitute a distillation of the life they conclude. For this reason, the passing of a religious figure is scrutinized with particular attention for signs of sanctity and indications of future rebirth. It may be noted, for instance, that one died quietly in meditation, or while practicing the yoga of *powa*. The unanticipated appearance of flowers out of season, pleasant aromas, lights in the heavens, and more may be regarded as omens. And of the innumerable signs that may accompany death, none is rarer or more marvelous than the disappearance of an adept in the "rainbow body" (*jalü*), the body of light. An oft-mentioned example is the death, in 1872, of the Nyingmapa master Pema Düdül.

Most religious figures, however, even those renowned for their accomplishments and sanctity, do not pass away so dramatically. Following their decease, their remains will often be preserved in state for some time, so that disciples and patrons from distant locations may arrive to pay last respects. Thus, as much as a year may intervene between death and cremation (for, to the best of my knowledge, the sky burial is seldom the means to dispose of the corpse of a distinguished cleric). During this period, the deceased is considered to repose in samādhi, and *powa* is usually not performed, for the saintly dead are thought to direct their own destinies without the interference of others. Following cremation, the ashes are carefully examined for hardened remains classed as relics (*ringsel*), some of which may be preserved in memorial

An adept's death

In the water ape year (1872), on the new moon of the peaceful month of Vaiśakha, the venerable lama [Pema Düdül] set up a meditation tent and dwelt there. He instructed his disciples to come, and had them all settle into meditation, [visualizing the guru] upon the crowns of their heads. . . . He then said, "Now, go back to your own places. After sewing shut my tent-flap, no one is to come here for seven days."

The disciples did what the lama had told them, and returned to their own places feeling mentally ill at ease. At dawn on the seventh day, they performed prostrations before the meditation tent which was the lama's dwelling, and they opened it up. The lord's robes and meditation seat, his hair and the nails of his fingers and toes were there on his bed, but the maṇḍala of his body had disappeared. At that, they lamented very much in sorrow, whereupon the sky was all filled by rainbow lights and such. At that time, some intelligent and supremely religious persons and some who were certainly his closest spiritual sons met him in contemplative experiences, visions, and dreams, in which he granted them his approval in speech, comforted them with the highest teachings, and so forth.

from the *Biography of Nyakla Pema Düdül*

stūpas, while some are distributed as blessings to disciples and sponsors, who carefully guard them as sacred treasures.

In some cases, too, a deceased master will be mummified rather than cremated, the preserved body encased in a stūpa as a relic unto itself and thus in effect transformed into a perpetual shrine. This was practiced, for instance, in the case of the Dalai Lamas, beginning with the fifth, whose gigantic, bejeweled memorial is housed in the Potala Palace in Lhasa. The mummification of noted spiritual leaders in Tibet may hark back to the ancient funerary rites of the rulers of the old Tibetan empire, though the precise connections between them remain to be studied in depth.

Postmortem journeys

An important class of mortuary specialist belongs at once to common and saintly spheres. Indeed, liminality is the hallmark of the *delok*, the revenant, who, in virtue of what we would term "near death experience," is uniquely stationed to offer testimony regarding the tribulations of those who traverse the *bardo* and the varied rebirths they attain. Such persons, who may have had no formal religious training before they "died," frequently act as diviners and healers following their experience, and written records of the *deloks*' travels in the beyond—whether fictional or based on the tales of historical revenants—are a popular form of religious literature. An example is the legend of Chöwang, a historical figure of the thirteenth century whose real biography contains no hint of this story of his otherworldly adventures.

Following his father's death and several failed attempts to convert his sinful mother, Chöwang departs to visit Lhasa on a business trip as the story unfolds. His mother dies before he returns home, leaving Chöwang tormented by anxious concern for her destiny. Entering a trance, he "dies" and ascends to heaven, where he meets the god Indra, who declares that, owing to his mother's arrogance and greed, she had quickly fallen from one realm to the one below. Realizing that his mother is to be found nowhere but in the hells, Chöwang meets with Yama, the lord of the dead, who urges him to give up his quest. But the hero persists and determines to take his mother's sufferings upon himself so that she be released. He is told, however, that the workings of karma are infallible, this being one of the messages that is highlighted throughout the *delok* literature. This moral is made clear through a series of judicial proceedings in Yama's court that unfold before Chöwang's eyes: A virtuous man who had once sinned—with three friends he once stole and slaughtered a yak—is mercifully sentenced to a series of human lives; a young woman, who had profited from her husband's trade as a diviner by deceiving those in distress, is condemned to a sealed iron chamber in the pit of hell; a preacher of Avalokiteśvara leads female disciples to higher rebirths, while most of their husbands descend; and the virtuous wife of a doctor is sentenced to just a week in the poisonous waters of purgatory in order to expiate her husband's crime of imprudently bleeding (in the medical sense) his patients.

After witnessing this, the fate of Chöwang's mother is at last revealed: she has been consigned to the sealed iron chamber in the very subbasement of hell. The hero manages to penetrate even this dungeon; his appearance there causes the demon-guardians to drop their weapons and faint, but at last he manages to find his mother among the shades. By reciting Avalokiteśvara's six-syllable mantra he secures the release of tens of thousands, but his mother remains incorrigible. Coercing her consciousness, he elevates her to the land of the hungry ghosts and from there to the animal realm. Following this, she is condemned to take birth once again, this time as a dog. In this form, she becomes receptive to her son's teaching of Dharma, and after returning with him to their ancestral home, she gives up her canine form to be reborn in the heavens where her former husband resides.

Such narratives pervade the *delok* literature. By offering first-person testimony in confirmation of the truths of karma and Buddhist cosmology, they serve to uphold the moral universe of Tibetan Buddhism, with its strongly marked distinctions of merit and fault.

Chapter 8
Tibetan Buddhism today

Twentieth-century developments

Early in 1912, following the fall of the Manchu Qing dynasty, the thirteenth Dalai Lama declared Tibetan independence. Although his vision embraced the vast region of Tibetan habitation that had been claimed by the government of the fifth Dalai Lama, the forces of Nationalist China and the warlords controlling its western provinces sought to consolidate Chinese rule in the eastern Tibetan regions of Kham and Amdo, and, indeed, continued to maintain that all Tibet belonged to China. The Dalai Lama succeeded in holding the territory corresponding to the actual Tibetan Autonomous Region, while Amdo mostly fell into China's Qinghai and Gansu provinces. In western Sichuan the new Chinese province of Xikang was created, corresponding to eastern Kham. Details aside, the status quo thus achieved reflected that which had prevailed under the Manchus, but with the important difference that the Dalai Lama now ruled an effectively independent state, if not one embracing the whole territory to which he aspired.

The division of Tibetan regions between China and a free Tibet had important entailments in the sphere of religion, whose ramifications are still felt to this day. While many Tibetan religious leaders, even within Chinese-controlled areas, remained loyal to the Dalai Lama and his government, others, who for one reason or another were disaffected, if not with the Dalai Lama personally then at least with his regime, decided to throw in their lot with the Nationalist Chinese. In some cases, for instance that of the ninth Panchen Lama Chökyi Nyima (1883–1937), who fled to China after a protracted dispute with the Lhasa authorities over taxation, this involved a real commitment to the principles of social and political modernization espoused by the founder of the Chinese Republic, Sun Yat-sen (1866–1925), and a desire to see similar progressive developments in Tibet. One result was a period of warm interchange between some Tibetan hierarchs and various groups in China: Chinese authorities in several provinces sponsored huge public ceremonies conducted by Tibetan lamas and monks, while ordinary Chinese devotees created Tibetan meditation centers in major cities including Shanghai and Chongqing, and noted Chinese Buddhist scholars became engaged in the study of Tibetan philosophical systems.

This background helps to explain why it was that when events in China turned in favor of the communists after World War II, some Tibetan modernists felt that the revolutionary programs of the Communist Party offered the best prospects for reform. Dobi Sherap Gyatso (1884–1968), for example, a renowned scholar who had had a stormy relationship with the thirteenth Dalai Lama, first joined the Chinese Nationalists but later turned to the communists. In 1952, two years after China assumed control of Tibet, he became the first chairman of the Chinese Buddhist Association. His attempt to find common ground between Communist Party policies and the interests of his religion was embraced by many educated Tibetan clergy during the 1950s, including both the present fourteenth Dalai Lama (b. 1935) and the tenth Panchen Lama (1938–89), who imagined that the ethical concerns of Mahāyāna Buddhism for universal well-being might be realized under Mao's socialist order.

It was not long, however, before the budding accord between Chinese communism and Tibetan Buddhism collapsed. As China's leaders came to regard the monasteries as inimical to reform, they grew openly more critical of religious leaders and institutions, and in 1956 some of the eastern Tibetan monasteries associated with rebel movements were bombed. Tibetans generally were horrified, and many from Amdo and Kham fled to Lhasa, where their swelling numbers helped to provoke the Lhasa Uprising of March 1959, followed by the Dalai Lama's self-imposed exile in India. Relations between the Tibetan Buddhist establishment and the Chinese government declined rapidly, and by 1962 the two most noted Tibetan religious figures remaining in China, the tenth Panchen Lama and Dobi Sherap Gyatso, proclaimed their disapproval of the government's handling of Tibetan affairs. In the years that followed, until the end of the Cultural Revolution (1966–76), religion was a principle target of the Communist Party's campaigns in Tibet: most of the several thousand temples and monasteries that had formerly existed were destroyed, their libraries and artwork dispersed or demolished, their monks and nuns—including prominent hierarchs such as the Panchen Lama—subjected to reeducation and harsh imprisonment, in which many perished.

While the disastrous conditions prevailing in China eliminated any scope for the open practice and transmission of Tibetan Buddhism, a Tibet-in-exile was being constructed under the Dalai Lama's leadership in India. In addition, communities that traditionally followed Tibetan Buddhism in the far north of India, as well as in Nepal and Bhutan, dedicated renewed energy to the preservation and development of their faith. This coincided with and helped to fuel a remarkable growth of interest in Tibetan Buddhism among Europeans, Americans, and overseas Chinese, with the ironic result that just as the tradition was eclipsed in its homeland, it began to garner a widespread international following.

Among the teachers who succeeded particularly well in promoting their traditions abroad were the head of the Nyingmapa order, Dudjom Rinpoché Jikdrel Yeshé Dorjé (1904–87), the sixteenth

Karmapa hierarch Rangjung Rikpé Dorjé (1924–81), the great eclectic master Dilgo Khyentsé Rinpoché Trashi Dawa (1910–91), and the master of the rare Shangpa Kagyü tradition Kalu Rinpoché Rangjung Künkhyap (1905–87), who succeeded in establishing a network of Western centers specializing in the traditional three-year retreat. A number of younger teachers, including Chögyam Trungpa Rinpoché (1939–87), Tarthang Tulku Rinpoché (b. 1934), Chögyal Namkhai Norbu (b. 1938), and Sogyal Rinpoché (b. 1947), became permanently installed in the United States or Europe, where they cultivated innovative approaches particularly geared to the background and interests of their Western disciples. The Bön religion also succeeded in gaining an international following, above all through the efforts of the charismatic scholar and meditation master, Loppön Tendzin Namdak (b. 1926).

The greatest success, however, was reserved for the fourteenth Dalai Lama, who assumed the role of an international spiritual superstar. Thanks to his abundant energy, personal integrity, openness to diverse cultures, and lively interest in dialogue of all kinds—religious, political, and scientific—the Dalai Lama was able to reach far beyond the relatively narrow range of Westerners motivated primarily by their involvement in Buddhism, and to engage in far-reaching conversations in a variety of fields, including interfaith dialogue, human rights, environmental issues, and the sciences. His worldwide popularity has been a great source of frustration to Chinese authorities, who regard him as a political renegade determined to split China apart, but, try though they may, they have not made much headway in convincing others that this is so.

Reform and retrenchment

Following the conclusion of the Cultural Revolution and Deng Xiaoping's rise to power in 1978, liberalization policies initiated in China began to transform the religious and cultural life of Tibet, and during the 1980s a remarkable upsurge of Buddhist activity ensued. The Panchen Lama, who by then had been freed from prison and rehabilitated, played a cardinal role here, encouraging the restoration or reconstruction of temples and monasteries wherever feasible, and urging the repatriation to Tibet of cultural treasures that had been taken to Beijing and elsewhere in eastern China during the preceding decades. The small numbers of surviving senior monks and nuns were augmented by a great many new novices, some entering the monasteries on their own but many, as in earlier times, sent by their families.

One of the several ironies stemming from the revival of Tibetan Buddhism in contemporary China has been its success as a spiritual movement among affluent and educated east-coast Chinese. The roots of this development may be found in part in the upsurge of Tibetan Buddhist activity in Nationalist China after the Qing dynasty and more immediately in the recent vogue of Tibetan Buddhism in Taiwan, Hong Kong, and elsewhere in overseas Chinese communities. Today eager students at leading universities in Beijing and Shanghai, much like their Western counterparts, fill classes on Tibetan Buddhism, and wealthy Chinese Buddhist devotees spend their vacations visiting teachers and temples in various parts of Tibet. Indeed, some of China's neo-Tibetan Buddhists, who have money, passports, and a measure of liberty that few of China's Tibetan citizens enjoy, regularly travel to India to meet with and receive teachings from leading masters in exile, including the Dalai Lama. Among Chinese students of Tibetan Buddhism, however, it is well understood that their religious engagement may be tolerated so long as it remains decisively apolitical.

While most Tibetan Buddhists in China, whatever their ethnicity, thus avoid mixing religion and politics, some in the clergy are assertive in their conviction that Tibetan religion and Tibetan autonomy are inevitably interlinked, and very large numbers of Tibetans remain privately loyal to the Dalai Lama. Beginning in the late 1980s, Tibet has been periodically rocked by protests and

10. In China, the practice of Tibetan Buddhism is now sometimes treated as a form of local folklore, attracting the attention of tourists and broadcast media.

riots in which the religious have played prominent roles, leading to ever-tightening restrictions on Tibetan religious activity. This has produced a paradoxical situation, paralleling patterns throughout China, in which the Chinese government permits and even promotes liberalizing trends, only to suffocate the ensuing expressions of freedom it regards as economically or politically inconvenient.

A series of significant crises erupted following the death, in 1989, of the highest ranking Tibetan hierarch in China, the Panchen Lama. Though some effort was made to coordinate the search for his successor, so that both the Dalai Lama and Chinese authorities might be in agreement, misunderstandings arose, and in May 1995 the Dalai Lama and the Tibetan government-in-exile independently announced the discovery of the young Panchen in Tibet. The Chinese reaction was livid, and the young boy, Gendun Choekyi Nyima, who had been recognized as the Panchen Lama by the Dalai Lama, was detained with his family, never to be heard from again. The Chinese government rejected his recognition and staged a lottery in November of the same year, choosing a new Panchen Lama from a slate of officially designated candidates.

Although Chinese authorities have attempted to legitimize their selection through a sustained publicity and propaganda campaign, China's Panchen has singularly failed to win the hearts and minds of the Tibetan people. This was most dramatically demonstrated in late 1999, when two of the leading Tibetan Buddhist figures in China—Arjia Rinpoché, the abbot of Kumbum monastery in Qinghai, and Urgyan Trinlay, one of two young lamas recognized as the seventeenth Karmapa incarnation—fled from China rather than acquiesce to the government's demand that they lend their affirmations to its recognition of the Panchen. (Arjia Rinpoché settled in the United States, while Urgyan Trinlay, effectively stealing the spotlight from a rival Karmapa, has become a close protégé of the Dalai Lama in India and has won a broad following among Tibetan exiles.)

Despite the involvement of numbers of mostly prosperous east-coast and overseas Chinese in Tibetan Buddhism, few of the many Chinese who have settled in Tibet for economic reasons have much interest in Tibetan religion and culture. Their economic dominance of the towns has come to be profoundly resented by Tibetans, particularly the youth, who suffer from high rates of unemployment. In March and April 2008, a series of violent demonstrations against the Chinese presence in Lhasa, in which numerous Chinese businesses were torched and individual Chinese attacked in the streets, provoked a firestorm of demonstrations throughout China's Tibetan regions. Not since 1959 had such widespread protest been seen. In parts of eastern Tibet, in particular, there was considerable monastic involvement, embroiling such prominent centers as Labrang Monastery in Gansu and Kirti Monastery in Sichuan. The Chinese response, which would have no doubt been harsh under any circumstances, was intensified by the negative attention these events created in the run-up to the 2008 Summer Olympics in Beijing, and in the aftermath of the Tibetan protests as many as one thousand monks were imprisoned. New restrictions were placed on many monasteries, and political education campaigns intensified.

Among the most tragic outcomes of the ongoing tensions over Tibetan affairs in China—in which the conditions of religious establishments and questions surrounding the status of the Dalai Lama play a major role—has been a significant number of self-immolations. Although beginning among Tibetan exiles in India as a manner of protesting Tibet's loss of independence, 2012–13 saw a wave of self-immolations, the majority involving monks or ex-monks, mostly in their teens or early twenties, from Kirti Monastery or nearby regions in the Tibetan districts of Sichuan, Gansu, and Qinghai. Tight restrictions on the monasteries in places in which ethnic Tibetans increasingly feel themselves to be losing ground to neighboring Chinese have no doubt contributed to the background conditions for such dramatic expressions of protest, but these events have yet to be fully explained. Notable, once again, is the role of the religious in relation to questions of Tibetan identity and autonomy.

In recent years, discussions of Tibetan Buddhism in the popular press have tended to be preoccupied with the question of the Dalai Lama's religious succession. (The Dalai Lama has already retired from his political functions, his succession in this respect having been determined in early 2011 by the election of Lobsang Sangay as prime minister of the Tibetan government-in-exile.) The topic has given rise to much ill-informed speculation, due in no small measure to the resistance on the part of the Dalai Lama himself to making public a clear succession plan. The issue is particularly delicate, because it is apparent that the government of China has its own plan: it will use its Panchen Lama to recognize a new Dalai Lama when the time comes, and, as it has done in the case of the Panchen Lama, it will impose this choice on the Tibetan people whatever their sentiments regarding its legitimacy may be. It is therefore incumbent upon the Dalai Lama and his partisans to arrive at a succession strategy that will effectively neutralize the Chinese effort.

It seems that it is due to the cat-and-mouse game in which the opposing parties are thus engaged that the Dalai Lama has opted to let a degree of uncertainty reign in regard to his real intentions: perhaps the identity of the next Dalai Lama will be decided while the present Dalai Lama is still alive; perhaps the Karmapa will be his successor; perhaps a citizen of India will be chosen as Dalai Lama; perhaps a woman. . . . In my view, none of these scenarios is very plausible; they have been allowed to float primarily because they create a quandary for the Chinese. The present Dalai Lama's imprimatur on any such option will have the effect of delegitimizing in advance, at least in the eyes of the Tibetan people (and it is *this* that is all-important), a Chinese attempt to have their Panchen Lama recognize the Dalai Lama's successor. The Dalai Lama's Tibetan followers in the end will most likely follow a traditional selection process, perhaps presided over by the Karmapa or another figure designated as the Dalai Lama's religious regent, and making sure that the procedure conforms with widespread Tibetan expectations.

The view from the West

Besides the Tibetan populations of China and South Asia, and others who have adhered to Tibetan Buddhism for centuries, including many Himalayan peoples and the Mongols of Russia, Mongolia, and China, Tibetan Buddhism today has achieved a modest following in many parts of the world. In Western countries, although some Tibetan Buddhist centers adhere closely to traditional models, there have also been significant innovations among them. The concern in Tibetan societies for merit-making, divinations, and apotropaic rituals, though not wholly absent, is reduced relative to a strong interest in the intellectual and contemplative facets of Buddhist teaching. (The disinclination of Westerners to participate in traditional merit-making is, for instance, evident in the practice of admitting participants to discourses and initiations on payment of a set fee rather than a voluntary donation.)

Particularly noteworthy is the prominent role of Tibetan Buddhist interlocutors, beginning with the Dalai Lama, in the ongoing dialogue between Buddhism and science (above all physics and the cognitive sciences). At the same time, Buddhist methods of contemplation have become an object of study among psychologists and others. (One major area of current scientific work is remarkable for its absence in these conversations, namely, evolutionary biology, which seems particularly difficult to reconcile with Buddhist conceptions of karma.) In some contexts, the religious content of Tibetan Buddhism is all but forgotten, and "Tibetan Buddhism" is reinscribed in contemporary settings as an option among therapies or self-realization techniques. Despite a pronounced tendency in the context of dialogue with the sciences to abstract Tibetan Buddhism from its ancestral religious framework, however, the Dalai Lama himself has remained an engaged participant in interreligious dialogue, urging that compassion, rather than the details of belief, be seen as a possible meeting-point among differing faiths.

Tibetan Buddhism has also served to involve Americans and Europeans in the Tibetan political cause, but this has been accomplished unevenly. It has contributed to the formation of vocal pro-Tibet lobbies in many countries, often allied with broader human rights organizations, ensuring that the Dalai

Lama regularly meets with national leaders and other prominent personalities. These activities infuriate Chinese leadership but yield few practical results; for China's importance in world affairs is such that no government will allow relations to be compromised on account of the Dalai Lama or the Tibet question. Polite meetings with him, and occasional legislative gestures of support, are, however, useful means for Western political figures to remind China of abiding human rights concerns, while throwing a bone to activists at home.

One may also note the rapidity with which Tibetan Buddhism in the West is becoming non-Tibetan. The translation of texts has assumed tidal proportions, so that for many adherents there is now no reason to learn the Tibetan language. Westerners who have completed lengthy retreats and programs of traditional study, some of whom sport the title of "lama," increasingly act as teachers among Western Buddhists, while a number of *trülkus* have been recognized in North America and Europe as well. Only time will tell whether Tibetan Buddhism will succeed in planting enduring roots in the West—even if in a form no longer quite Tibetan—or whether it will prove to be a passing trend. For the present writer, in any case, the chief interest of this tradition remains its long, endlessly varied, and intricately refined development within the splendid civilization of Tibet.

References and further reading

The author's *The Tibetans* (Oxford: Blackwell, 2006) surveys Tibetan history and culture, and includes a detailed bibliography. *Sources of Tibetan Tradition*, ed. Kurtis Schaeffer, Matthew Kapstein, and Gray Tuttle (New York: Columbia University Press, 2013) provides translated selections from almost two hundred works. The Library of Tibetan Classics, published by Wisdom Publications, provides authoritative, complete translations of major works representing all schools of Tibetan Buddhism.

The following notes specify the sources of citations throughout this work, with additional reading recommendations. Unless otherwise mentioned, all translations are the author's.

Chapter 1

Quotations from "a twelfth-century Bön text" are based on my "The *Commentaries of the Four Clever Men*: A Doctrinal and Philosophical Corpus in the Bon po *rDzogs chen* Tradition," *East & West* 59 (2009): 107–30. For Zurchungpa, see Dudjom Rinpoche Jikdrel Yeshe Dorje, *The Nyingma School of Tibetan Buddhism: Its Fundamentals and History*, trans. Gyurme Dorje and Matthew Kapstein, 2nd ed. (Boston: Wisdom Publications, 2002), 1:629. The *sang* liturgy is translated from the *Ri bo bsang mchod* of Lha-btsun Nam-mkha'-'jigs-med.

Geoff Childs, *Tibetan Diary: From Birth to Death and Beyond in a Himalayan Valley of Nepal* (Berkeley: University of California Press, 2004) is an outstanding introduction to the ethnography of Tibetan Buddhism. For a broad survey of the anthropological literature, see

Geoffrey Samuel, *Civilized Shamans: Buddhism in Tibetan Societies* (Washington, DC: Smithsonian Institution Press, 1993). Per Kværne, *The Bon Religion of Tibet* (London: Serindia Publications, 1995) offers an accessible introduction to Bön. Donald S. Lopez Jr., ed., *Religions of Tibet in Practice* (Princeton, NJ: Princeton University Press, 1997) provides an anthology relating to ritual, pilgrimage, meditation, etc.

Chapter 2

Selections from Tri Songdetsen's edicts and the Samyé debate are from my "Buddhist Thought in Tibet: An Historical Introduction," in *The Oxford Handbook of World Philosophies*, ed. William Edelglass and Jay L. Garfield (New York: Oxford University Press, 2011), 244–62. The discussion of the vehicles from the *Lta ba'i khyad par* of Ye-shes-sde is presented here for the first time. The "early text in which 'Bön' unambiguously denotes the pre-Buddhist religion" is edited and translated in Pasang Wangdu and Hildegard Diember-ger, *dBa' bzhed: The Royal Narrative Concerning the Bringing of the Buddha's Doctrine to Tibet* (Vienna: Österreichische Akademie der Wissenschaften, 2000). The extract from Tri Desongtsen's edict on tantric practice and the summary of the nine vehicles are from my *The Tibetan Assimilation of Buddhism: Conversion, Contestation, and Memory* (New York: Oxford University Press, 2000).

Chapter 3

Ronald M. Davidson, *Tibetan Renaissance* (New York: Columbia University Press, 2005) studies the period of the post–tenth-century revival of Tibetan Buddhism with particular attention to the Sakyapa. For the "eight lineages," refer to my "gDams-ngag: Tibetan Technologies of the Self," in *Tibetan Literature: Studies in Genre*, ed. Roger Jackson and José Cabezón (Ithaca, NY: Snow Lion Publications, 1995), 275–89; and "Tibetan Technologies of the Self, Part 2," in Ramón Prats, ed., *The Pandita and the Siddha* (Dharamsala: Amnye Machen Research Institute, 2007), 110–29.

Chapter 4

The "elegy of worship" comes from my "The Guide to the Crystal Peak: A Pilgrim's Handbook," in D. Lopez, *Tibetan Religions in Practice*, 103–19. On pilgrimage, see Toni Huber, *The Cult of Pure Crystal*

Mountain (New York: Oxford University Press, 1998). Translations
from the writings of Atiśa throughout the chapter are my own.
Pakpa's "letter of spiritual advice" is cited from my "Chos-rgyal
'Phags-pa's Advice to a Mongolian Noblewoman," in *Historical
and Philological Studies of China's Western Regions* 3 (2010):
135–43. Verses from the *Maṇi Kabum* are from my "The Royal
Way of Supreme Compassion," in D. Lopez, ed., *Tibetan Religions
in Practice*, 69–76.

Thupten Jinpa, *Mind Training: The Great Collection* (Boston:
Wisdom, 2006) is a superb collection of the major works of the
lojong genre.

Chapter 5

The "nineteenth-century teacher from Amdo" is Düjom Dorjé,
on whom see my "The Sprul-sku's Miserable Lot: Critical
Voices from Eastern Tibet," in *Amdo Tibetans in Transition*,
ed. Toni Huber (Leiden: Brill, 2002), 99–111. Citations from
Karma Pakshi, Karmapa Rangjung Dorjé, Dölpopa, Longchen
Rapjampa, Tsongkhapa, and Mipam are based on my "Buddhist
Thought in Tibet," in Edelglass and Garfield, *Oxford Handbook
of World Philosophies*. The passage from Sakya Paṇḍita is
translated here from his *Skyes bu dam pa la spring ba*. The
quotation from Gorampa is based on the translation of José
Cabezón and Geshe Lobsang Dargyay, *Freedom from Extremes:
Gorampa's "Distinguishing the Views" and the Polemics of
Emptiness* (Boston: Wisdom, 2007), 137.

For a thorough account of Tibetan monastic education, see Georges
B. J. Dreyfus, *The Sound of Two Hands Clapping: The Education
of a Tibetan Buddhist Monk* (Berkeley: University of California
Press, 2003). Tuken's great synthesis of Indian, Tibetan, and
Chinese philosophy is now available in a fine English translation:
Geshe Lhundup Sopa and Roger R. Jackson, eds. and trans., *The
Crystal Mirror of Philosophical Systems: A Tibetan Study of Asian
Religious Thought* (Boston: Wisdom, 2009).

Chapter 6

Peltrül Rinpoché's discussion of the "characteristics of Buddhist
tantra" may be found in his beautiful introduction to Nyingmapa
tantric practice, translated in Padmakara Translation Committee,
The Words of My Perfect Teacher (San Francisco: Harper Collins,

1994). The traditional account of Milarepa's discipleship is Tsangnyön Heruka, *The Life of Milarepa*, trans. Andrew Quintman (New York: Penguin, 2010). Quotations from Sachen Künga Nyingpo's *Rgyud sde spyi rnam* are translated here for the first time. The verse by Karmapa Rangjung Dorjé is from his *Phyag chen smon lam* ("Mahāmudrā Prayer").

Chapter 7

Part of this chapter is based on my *The Tibetan Assimilation of Buddhism*. The "fourteenth-century 'treasure' attributed to Padmasambhava" is the *Gdam ngag mar gyi yang zhun gdam pa 'chi ba'i ngo sprod* revealed by Rdo-rje-gling-pa. For the sleep meditation by Sakya Paṇḍita, see my "Pure Land Buddhism in Tibet?" in *Approaching the Land of Bliss: Religious Praxis in the Cult of Amitabha*, ed. Richard Payne and Kenneth Tanaka (University of Hawai'i Press, 2004), 16–41; and on the death of Pema Düdül, my "The Strange Death of Pema the Demon-Tamer," in *The Presence of Light*, ed. Matthew T. Kapstein (Chicago: University of Chicago Press, 2004), 119–56. The legend of Chöwang is based on my "Mulian in the Land of Snows and King Gesar in Hell: A Chinese Tale of Parental Death in Its Tibetan Transformations," in *The Buddhist Dead: Practices, Discourses, Representations*, ed. Bryan J. Cuevas and Jacqueline I. Stone (Honolulu: University of Hawai'i Press, 2007), 345–77.

Gyurme Dorje, trans., *The Tibetan Book of the Dead*, ed. Graham Coleman with Thupten Jinpa (New York: Viking, 2006) provides the fullest selection from the famous "Book" in English. Bryan J. Cuevas, *Travels in the Netherworld* (New York: Oxford University Press, 2008) offers an attractive selection of *delok* tales.

Chapter 8

Early twentieth-century relations between Tibetan and Chinese Buddhists are studied in Gray Tuttle, *Faith and Nation: Tibetan Buddhists in the Making of Modern China* (New York: Columbia University Press, 2005); and in several of the chapters of my edited volume, *Buddhism Between Tibet and China* (Boston: Wisdom Publications, 2009). Case studies in Tibetan Buddhism during the 1980s and '90s may be found in Melvyn C. Goldstein and Matthew T. Kapstein, eds., *Buddhism in Contemporary Tibet: Religious Revival and Cultural Identity* (Berkeley: University of California Press, 1998). Donald S. Lopez Jr., *Prisoners of Shangri-la: Tibetan Buddhism and the West* (Chicago: University of Chicago Press, 1998) provides an entertaining account of Western engagements in Tibetan Buddhism, while his *Buddhism and Science: A Guide for the Perplexed* (Chicago: University of Chicago Press, 2008) surveys many areas of recent dialogue between Buddhism and science, with particular emphasis on the role of Tibetan Buddhism therein.

Video and Internet Resources

Videos available on DVD

Destroyer of Illusion: The Secret World of a Tibetan Lama. Dir. Richard Kohn. 1991/2006. Festival Media. An engrossing ethnographic film documenting the Mani Rimdu festival in Nepal, with its elaborate rites of masked dance.

The Lion's Roar. Dir. Mark Elliot. 1985/2006. Festival Media. A moving portrait of the sixteenth Karmapa.

Milarepa: Magician, Murderer, Saint. Dir. Neten Chokling. 2008. Shining Moon Productions. Compelling interpretation of Milarepa's early life, his career as a black magician, filmed in Tibetan from a distinctively Tibetan perspective. A sequel, following Milarepa's discipleship under Marpa, is promised.

The Reincarnation of Khensur Rinpoche. Dir. Ritu Saran and Tenzin Sonam. 1991/1999. White Crane. Outstanding record of the search for a deceased master's reincarnation.

The Saltmen of Tibet. Dir. Ulrike Koch. 1997/2002. Zeitgeist Films. Stunning documentation of the occupations and rituals of the salt-gatherers of far western Tibet.

Tibet: A Buddhist Trilogy. Dir. Graham Coleman. 1979/2006. Festival Media. Trilogy filmed in Nepal, India, and Ladakh, introducing the Dalai Lama, tantric meditation practices, and mortuary rites.

Tibetan Buddhism: Preserving the Monastic Tradition. Dir. Edward Bastian. 1982. University of Wisconsin. Introduction to monastic life in the refugee monastery of Sera in South India.

The Yogis of Tibet: A Film for Posterity. Dir. Phil and Jo Borack. 2002. JEHM Films. A remarkable encounter with adepts of the esoteric techniques of tantric yoga.

Websites

Himalayan Art Resources (http://www.himalayanart.org/). The world's largest educational resource for Himalayan Art and iconography.

The Tibetan and Himalayan Library (THL) (http://www.thlib.org/). A publisher of websites, information services, and networking facilities relating to the Tibetan plateau and southern Himalayan regions.

The Treasury of Lives: Biographies of Himalayan Religious Masters (http://www.treasuryoflives.org/). A bibliographical encyclopedia of all known past masters of Himalayan religion, both Buddhist and Bon.

Tibetan Buddhist Resource Center (http://www.tbrc.org/). The Tibetan Buddhist Resource Center (TBRC) is dedicated to seeking out, preserving, organizing, and disseminating Tibetan literature.

Index

Index

Index